10 MINUTES TO BECOME A BETTER PARENT

MUSFIRA ANSARI

TRUE SIGN
PUBLISHING HOUSE

Published by True Sign Publishing House
Address: SY. No. 21/2 & 21/3, Sonnenahalli,
Krishnarajapura, Bengaluru,
Karnataka - 560049 India
E-mail: truesignbooks@gmail.com
Website: www.truesign.in

10 Minutes To Become A Better Parent

Author: Musfira Ansari

ISBN:978-93-5805-338-8

First Edition: 2023

CONTENTS

Extracted formula of parenting

Parenting is about being present. Parenting involves more than just completing a task, selecting the best form of discipline, or creating a contributing member of society. Effective, God-honoring parenting essentially entails building an intimate, trustworthy, and expanding relationship with a child, as Scripture confirms as well as ample statistical and anecdotal experience. Everyone tries to determine how the relationship between parents and children can develop into the ideal one when it comes to family life. Every parent's ideal is to raise their children to be well-behaved, disciplined adults who have strong moral principles. But it is not a simple task. Furthermore, it is crucial to understand that the parent-child relationship is a partnership between a parent and their child and operates on a two-way street. When a garden of various flowers blooms, it becomes beautiful. Similar to this, a parent's "garden" will become fragrant if they learn how to be a "gardener" and recognize and nurture their child's personality. Positive parenting is all about this. Parents who master good parenting techniques and fill the generational gap on their own. Children won't become spoiled when parents learn to strike a balance between setting boundaries and encouraging and discouraging behavior. This helps them become better parents. Distance between the two grows when people slack parenting skills.

1. Your actions matter

Your children are watching what you do, whether it's how you treat other people or how you conduct yourself in terms of your own health. "This is one of the most crucial principles," Your actions have an impact... Avoid simply responding on the spur of the moment. Consider what you want to achieve and whether doing this will help you get there. Your child learns from your actions. They learn how to behave in a certain situation by watching you. So, before you jump into action, think about the impression you will leave on your child.

2. You can never love too much

Simply put, "you can't spoil a kid." There is no such thing as too much love for a child, despite what many people think. Contrary to popular belief, a child can never experience too much love. It is usually the result of giving a child something other than love, such as indulgence, lowered standards, or material possessions. Instead, compliment your child when they achieve something, tell them they did good work and motivate them to do better.

3. Participate in your kid's life

Effort and time are required from involved parents, and it frequently involves reevaluating and rearranging your responsibilities. It frequently demonstrates giving up your desires in favor of what your child needs. Be present both mentally and physically. Being involved does not entail doing or checking a child's homework. If you do the homework, you're not letting the teacher know what the child is learning. Homework is a tool for teachers to determine if the child is learning or not. Let them make mistakes and learn from them. It will help them grow and develop their personalities.

4. Make parenting adjustments to fit your child's

Follow your child's development closely. Your child is developing. Consider how age is affecting the child's behavior.

The same desire for independence that makes your 3-year-old say "no," all the time is what's driving them to be potty trained. The parent said, "Your 13-year-old's argumentative behavior at the dinner table is the result of the same intellectual growth spurt that makes them curious in the classroom."

5. Make rules and establish them

If you do not control your child's behavior when they are young, they will struggle to learn self-control when they are older and you are not around. You should always be able to respond to these three inquiries, day or night. Where is my kid exactly? Who is my child with? What's my kid up to? The rules your child applies to himself will be shaped by the rules they have learned from you.

But you cannot micromanage your child. You must stop interfering once the child is in middle school and allow them to complete their own homework and make their own decisions.

6. Encourage your child's independence

"Setting boundaries aids in a child's self-control development." They gain a sense of self-direction by being supported by their independence. To be successful in life, they're going to need both.

It's common for kids to demand independence. Many parents incorrectly associate their child's independence with disobedience or rebellion. Children demand independence because it is human nature to prefer feeling in control to feeling controlled by others.

7. Be reliable

Your child's misbehavior is not their fault; it is your fault if your rules change from day to day unpredictably or if you only occasionally enforce them. The most important tool you have for discipline is consistency. Establish what's forbidden. Your child will be less inclined to challenge your authority if they found it on knowledge rather than strength.

8. Prevent using severe punishment

Parents should never hit a child, under any circumstances. Children who are spanked, hit, or slapped are more prone to fighting with other children. They are more likely to bully others and resort to violence to settle disagreements with other people.

"There are a lot of other, more effective ways to discipline a child, including 'time out,' which do not involve violence,"

9. Describe your guidelines and judgments

Good parents have standards they want their children to live up to. Parents explain things too much to young children and not enough to teenagers. A 12-year-old might not see what you do as being obvious. Compare to you, they lack your experience, judgment, and priorities.

10. Show respect to your children

"Treating your child respectfully is the best way to instill respect in them." The same decency you would extend to anyone else should be extended to your child. Speak to them politely. Respect their viewpoint. When they speak to you, pay attention. Show them respect. When you can, try to please them. Children behave toward others as they would like to be treated. The foundation of your child's relationships with others is your relationship with them.

In the case of a picky eater, for instance, I do not think parents should make a big deal about eating. Children form dietary preferences. They often go through them in stages. Avoid making meals uncomfortable for yourself and others. Just do not substitute unhealthy foods, that would be a mistake. Do not keep junk food in the house, instead replace it with healthy snacks slowly.

The Routines of Highly Effective Parents

Making mistakes is a given when you become a parent. At least occasionally, you will say the wrong thing, choose the incorrect course of action, or arrive at the incorrect time.

Additionally, count on your child yelling at you, making fun of you, and becoming irritated with you at various points. All of those blunders and responses are typical.

But trying to be the ideal parent should not be your goal; it's just not possible. Furthermore, you don't have to be flawless to be a good parent. Your child can learn important lessons from your errors, misfortunes, and gaffes.

The best parents strive to raise a child who is responsible, mentally strong, and prepared for the realities of adulthood. Here are nine practices used by extremely successful parents to achieve that goal.

1. Follow the regulations

In addition to helping you stay sane, house rules and boundaries give a growing child a sense of stability and security. A good parent makes it clear to their children what they can and cannot do, what tasks they must complete, and how they should interact with other family members (including pets).

Of course, every kid makes mistakes now and then. Use an if... then warning after giving your child instructions. You won't be able to go to the park if you don't put your toys right away. This step demonstrates to your child that, while making mistakes is acceptable, they are still accountable for their subsequent actions.

If they disobey a key rule—like hitting you—make sure the repercussions are immediate. Show them it is your responsibility to teach them to follow the rules and that the purpose of the consequences is to help them learn from their mistakes.

10 MINUTES TO BECOME A BETTER PARENT

2. They Continue to Be Flexible

There are two types of enforcing the law: reasonable and excessively strict. For certain circumstances, you need to keep a little flexibility on hand.

Too many rules could have unintended consequences. According to a University of New Hampshire study, parents who are overly strict actually raise kids who are more likely to disobey the rules.

Additionally, studies reveal that kids with extremely strict parents frequently have lower self-esteem and a diminished sense of self-worth than kids with parents who occasionally let loose.

In general, your child should be aware of the repercussions of breaking certain rules, but effective discipline isn't always a clear-cut matter. As your family grows, the kids get older, and circumstances change, modify the rules and the punishment.

3. They Interact with Their Children

Effective communication is the first step to effective parenting. Children gain from talking to their parents, even when they are still learning how to babble.

Talk about anything and everything, including your day at school, the upcoming baseball season, and what he wants for his birthday this year. No subject should be taboo.

The benefits for your children increase as you spend more time conversing with them. It teaches them about language, interpersonal skills, and creative thinking.

Regular conversations also help your child feel more secure and loved because they demonstrate your interest in what they have to say. As a result, if you talk to your child frequently when they are young, they will be more likely to do so when they are an adult.

4. Reading to Children

Talking to your child more frequently and doing this go hand in hand. Your child will learn new vocabulary, understand various ideas, and enter new worlds as a result of reading aloud to him.

If your child prefers nonfiction books, they will have access to a wealth of facts as well as a better understanding of grammatical structures.

In addition, they will have a stronger imagination if you read to them frequently.

A study by the Organization for Economic Cooperation and Development found that parents who read aloud to their children when they were young were up to a year ahead of their academic peers by the time, they were 15 years old. Aim to read to your child individually for at least 20 minutes each day.

5. They Share Quality Time

In the course of a typical day, you must spend a lot of time with your child, right? After all, you both commute to work and school together, you share a meal tonight, and you tuck them in at night.

However, none of these amounts to the amount of quality time a child needs to grow with their parents. Give your child 10 to 15 minutes of your undivided attention each day so that he can participate in an activity of his choosing.

Play a game, pretend to be someone else, or take a run. Giving your child a lot of time inside will probably cut down on the time he spends in time-out.

6. They Let Children Take on Challenges

Although adversity helps to develop character, it is still difficult to watch your child struggle. There will always be situations where your little one needs your help—or even a bailout of some sort. As he gets older, take a step back to see how he conquers the challenges he faces on his own.

Don't jump in and ask team leadership to make things right. For instance, your child has been working hard to be named the pitcher on the Little League team and the coach chooses someone else to start the game.

Tell your child that despite your best efforts, things don't always turn out as you had hoped. Encourage him to keep improving so he can try again the following year.

This method teaches kids that sometimes things don't work their way—but that's no reason to give up—and that their parents won't always solve their problems. Teach your child healthy coping mechanisms for difficult emotions like failure and rejection.

7. They Value Their Child's Independence Needs

At the age of two, a child starts to learn how to make their own decisions, and they frequently express them loudly. As they get older, those choices will matter more.

Even if you disagree with the decisions, you should respect them (provided that doing so won't seriously endanger the safety of your child or another person; use your judgment in this regard). Recognize that something may not be the wrong idea just because they don't do it the way you might.

Your child will learn that decisions can have consequences if they make that choice, even if it doesn't turn out well. If it does turn out well for them, they will discover the benefits of making wise choices for their future.

Therefore, occasionally let your child experience natural consequences. Allow them to walk outside without a coat if they insist on doing so and there is no risk of them getting too cold. They'll be more likely to wear their jacket the next time they get cold.

8. They Take Vacations Away from Their Children

It's normal to think of your children as the center of the universe and your entire existence. But that doesn't mean you have to be there for them every minute of every day, every year.

Sometimes parents need a break. Plan some time away from your kids so you can take care of yourself or your relationship.

Don't let others dictate what is acceptable and what is not; you (and your partner) get to decide how much time you need and when you need it. On Sunday mornings, your partner may leave the house with the kids. Therefore, you can sleep in, enjoy a cup of coffee in peace, and browse the internet at your leisure.

Another option is to plan a date night with a babysitter once a month so you can reconnect over a meal for two. Don't forget to take occasional nights off by asking a grandparent, sibling, or reliable friend to watch your children.

It's healthy to show your child that you have interests, hobbies, and activities outside of the house. And taking a break now and then will show them that they can survive without you.

9. They Have Unconditional Love for Their Children

They shouldn't feel as though they have to earn your favor, and your love for them shouldn't be restricted or limited. No matter how many mistakes the kids make, effective parents make it clear that they will always be there for them.

As their child develops, they give him or her love, support, and direction. The ultimate goal of parenting is to see your child grow up to be a happy, responsible adult.

Don't forget to give your child praise when they are doing well. Praise them instead for their willingness to try their finest or for their desire to try again if they fail. Make sure your child understands that your love for them is independent of their accomplishments and success. Show them that you still care about them.

When babies perceive themselves through their parents' eyes, they begin to establish a sense of self. Your children pick up on your tone of voice, body language, and facial expressions. More than anything else, your words and actions as a parent influence their developing self-esteem.

Praise for accomplishments, no matter how minor, will help them feel proud; allowing children to do things on their own will make them more capable and powerful. Belittling comments or unfair comparisons of one child to another, on the other hand, will make children feel worthless.

Avoid using words as weapons or making loaded assertions. Comments such as "What a silly thing to do!" or "You act more like a baby than your tiny brother!" can cause just as much damage as physical strikes.

Choose your words wisely. Have you ever considered how many times you react adversely to your children on a given day? You could find yourself criticising more than complimenting. How would you feel if your supervisor gave you that much harsh criticism, even if it was well-intended?

The most successful strategy is to catch children doing something right: "You made your bed without being asked—fantastic!" or "I was watching you play with your sister and you were extremely patient." In the long term, these words will do more to encourage good behaviour than repeated scolding.

Every day, make it a point to discover something to praise. Be liberal with your rewards—love, hugs, and compliments can do wonders and are frequently rewarded.

　　　　10 MINUTES TO BECOME A BETTER PARENT

Every household needs discipline. The purpose of discipline is to teach children acceptable behaviour and self-control. Kids may test the boundaries you set for them, but they need those boundaries to mature into responsible individuals.

Making house rules teaches children about your expectations and helps them develop self-control. Some ground rules might be: no TV until homework is completed; no hitting, name-calling, or nasty teasing permitted.

You might want to implement a system that includes a single warning followed by repercussions such as "time out" or loss of rights. Failure to follow through with repercussions is a common mistake made by parents. You can't discipline them one day and then neglect them the next. Consistency teaches us what to anticipate.

It is frequently difficult for parents and children to gather for a family meal, let alone spend quality time together. But there's nothing more appealing to children. Get up 10 minutes earlier to enjoy breakfast with your child, or leave the dishes in the sink and set out for a walk after supper. Children who do not receive the attention they desire from their parents may act out or misbehave in order to be acknowledged.

Many parents find it rewarding to schedule time with their children. Make a "special night" for your family each week and let your children decide how to spend the time. Look for alternative ways to connect – send a letter or something.

Adolescents appear to require less undivided attention from their parents than younger children do. Because there are limited opportunities for parents and teens to interact, parents should make every effort to be present. This is because their teen expresses a desire to communicate or join in family activities. Attending concerts, games, and other events with your teen displays care and allows you to learn more about your child and his or her pals.

If you're a working parent, don't feel ashamed of it. Kids will remember the many small things you do, such as preparing popcorn, playing cards, taking them window shopping.

Young children pick up a lot about how to act from their parents. The younger they are, the more they will pick up on your cues. Before you lash out or lose your cool in front of your child, consider this: Is this how you want your child to act when he or she is angry? Be mindful that your children are continuously watching you. According to studies, children who are hit usually have an aggressive role model at home.

Model the qualities you want your children to have: respect, friendliness, honesty, kindness, and tolerance. Demonstrate selflessness. Do things for others without expecting anything in return. Thank you and provide praise. Above all, treat your children the way you want others to treat you.

You cannot expect children to accomplish everything simply because you, as a parent, expect them to "say so. "Children, like adults, seek and deserve explanations. Children will begin to question our beliefs and reasons if we do not take the time to explain them. Reasoning with children allows them to understand and learn in a non-judgmental manner.

Make it clear what you anticipate. If there is a problem, describe it, share your thoughts, and allow your child to collaborate with you on a solution. Include the ramifications. Make suggestions and provide options. Be open to your child's ideas as well. Negotiate. Children who are involved in decision-making are more likely to carry them out.

If you frequently feel "let down" by your child's behavior, it's possible that you have unreasonable expectations. Parents who think in terms of "shoulds" (for example, "My kid should be potty-trained by now") may benefit from reading more on the subject or speaking with other parents or child development specialists.

Because children's environments influence their conduct, you may be able to alter that behavior by changing the environment. If you find yourself saying "no" to your 2-year-old all the time, look for methods to change your environment so that fewer things are off-limits. This will make things easier for both of you.

Your parenting approach will have to evolve as your child grows. What works for your child now may not work as well in a year or two.

Teens look to their peers for role models rather than their parents. However, continue to provide advice, encouragement, and appropriate discipline while your teen gains independence. And take advantage of every opportunity to connect! Parents are responsible for correcting and guiding their children.

However, how you express remedial feedback greatly influences how the child perceives it. When confronting your child, avoid accusing, condemning, or finding fault, as these actions erode self-esteem and can lead to resentment. Instead, even when disciplining your children, try to nourish and encourage them. Make it clear to them that, while you hope and expect better the next time, your love is always present. Face it: you are a flawed parent. As a family leader, you have both strengths and weaknesses. Recognize your strengths—"I am caring and dedicated." Make a commitment to improving your weaknesses—"I need to be more consistent with discipline." Try to set reasonable goals for yourself, your spouse, and your children. You don't have to know all the answers – just be patient. And make parenting a manageable task. Rather than attempting to cover everything at once, concentrate on the areas that require the most attention. When you're exhausted, admit it. Take time away from parenting to do things that make you happy as an individual (or as a couple).

You are not selfish if you prioritize your needs. It just indicates you are concerned about your personal well-being, which is an important value to instill in your children.

Growing up involves a crucial and natural process of gaining independence and doing more and more things on your own. But what can parents do to ensure that their children are receiving the encouragement and, if necessary, the prodding they need to develop self-assurance and independence?

Kids can be encouraged to be more independent and responsible in a variety of contexts, which is often overlooked in discussions about "free-range kids." At age 6, your child can learn independence in other ways besides just playing in a public park or walking to school by themselves.

It is unfair to refer to parents as "helicopter parents" if they want to, for example, walk an 8-year-old to school. The family in question might reside close to busy streets, the child might not be old enough to cross those streets alone, or the parents might simply value the time they spend together while walking their children to school.

Regardless of their feelings regarding young children being left alone in the outdoors, parents can promote independence in school-age children in a variety of ways. You can encourage independence in a number of ways.

Performing household duties: Your child should be able to handle age-appropriate household tasks, from sweeping floors to washing dishes, depending on how reliable and focused they can be. Even young children can help organize their rooms or set dining tables. Children learn responsibility from doing chores, and they may feel more confident as they see how their labor benefits the family.

Even though the simple household chores your 5-year-old can handle may not seem like much, they can teach your child priceless lessons that will stick with him through his preteen years and beyond. Your grade-schooler can contribute significantly to household tasks by the time they are 9 or 10 years old. Here are some instances of how chores can be advantageous for kids:

Giving kids chores can build self-esteem. When a task is successfully completed, when a task is successfully completed, your child may experience a strong sense of accomplishment. Every weekend, a 7-year-old uses a microfiber cloth to vacuum and clean the floor. When they are not in the mood to work, they occasionally complain, but once they start, they usually get into it. Furthermore, the fact that they are succeeding on their own promotes independence. And the expression on their face when they successfully manage to corral dust bunnies is priceless.

Giving kids chores can teach them the importance of completing an assigned job. Giving children chores can help them learn the value of finishing a task. This will become more useful as your child gets older and has more responsibilities at school and at home.

Giving kids chores emphasizes the value of keeping things clean and organized. When your environment is less cluttered, it's simpler to find things and think clearly. When your environment is less cluttered, finding things and thinking clearly are both made easier. Getting your child into the habit of regularly picking up after themselves is a great way to not only build a healthy routine that will benefit them for the rest of their life, but will help you keep cutting out the chaos in your house and making it more organized and peaceful.

Giving kids chores can set a pattern for helping around the house. Giving children chores can encourage them to assist around the house. Once you've ingrained the habit of doing the dishes, your child will continue to practice it well into adulthood. Beyond. If they instils the habit of doing the dishes, your children will carry it with them through their teen years and beyond. Part of their life that will continue into their teen years and beyond.

Giving kids chores can give them a sense of being part of the household team. When your children asks why they must complete a task, you should respond that they are a member of the family, and each member is required to complete their fair share. They more likely to see their work as a component of something bigger by being given the perspective that "we're all in this together." They are also less likely to see household chores as something they're being singled out and forced to do since everyone is working together.

Putting together menus and going grocery shopping:

One of the finest things you can do for your child is teach them how to prepare straightforward meals and feel at ease in the kitchen. Families can spend quality time together while shopping and cooking, which is a great way to instill in children a love of healthy food.

They talk a lot about themselves and what's going on in their lives when you and your kids are doing routine activities like grocery shopping, cooking, or eating together. To help your child become more independent, let them help prepare family meals and snacks—and eventually let them occasionally take the reins.

The upbringing of younger siblings and other children. Having children take care of younger children is one of the best ways to teach them how to be mature and responsible. The best babysitters in the area will likely be dependable, responsible, and compassionate teenagers, so look around you for them. Each family can decide what "babysitting" entails for a child of school age: Another family might decide it's okay to leave a 10-year-old with a 7-year-old sibling while the parent runs to the store for a few minutes. One family might want their 9-year-old to be in charge of reading or playing games with a younger sibling while a grown-up is nearby.A great way to encourage children to become more independent and responsible is to entrust an older child with the care of younger children..

Attending Solo Social Events

As children get older, it goes without saying that they spend more time doing things on their own away from home. There will be more birthday celebrations that are open to children in school. They will play alone at friends' houses with less close parental supervision, choose the games they'll play themselves more often, and resolve conflicts on their own.

Set up play dates at your house for your child if they're ready, and let them pick the activities they might want to recommend to their friends. Inform them that visiting friends' homes will be enjoyable and that you will be able to share and discuss your day with them when you pick them up. (However, make sure to check that safety is a top priority by asking questions before you leave your child with a friend.)

Be encouraging rather than critical and encourage your child to keep trying if they feel awkward or unprepared.

Volunteering

Everything is naturally about the needs and desires of very young children. Children who lend a hand to others develop empathy, which is a crucial step on the road to adulthood.

If your children volunteer, whether it's to make sandwiches for needy families at church or assist an elderly neighbor, they will be less likely to become spoiled or experience affluenza and more likely to develop into kind and compassionate adults as they get older.

Monitoring Assignments and Tests

It's one thing to assist your first-grader in organizing their homework and in creating the habit of noting when they have to study for tests. If a typically developing child in middle or high school requires parental assistance in keeping track of their schoolwork, that is something entirely different.

Establishing good work habits early will help your child learn to manage their responsibilities on their own as they get older and lessen the need for you to constantly remind them when and what to do for school.

You're not the only one who struggles with homework completion in your home or who has daily arguments about allocating enough time for homework. Therefore, teachers advise parents to create a homework schedule with their children's input.

There won't be any doubts about when the homework will be finished once you've established a schedule. It also conveys clear expectations; giving children a homework schedule makes it easier for them to understand what is expected of them. Additionally, sticking to the schedule motivates them to cultivate a strong work ethic.

Additionally, schedules encourage positive habits like finishing work on time and help stop procrastination. Routines for doing homework help kids learn how to study and encourage them to make plans.

The improvement of your child's work ethic and organizational skills are additional advantages. You are teaching your child how to manage time and projects in the future by helping them finish their work on a regular basis. They will be able to pace their work when you send them off to college, preventing all-nighters at the end of the semester.

To create a schedule for homework, start by discussing it with your children. Ask for their opinions on the best ways to organize their time and fit homework into their daily schedule. A productive homework schedule enables students to complete their assignments and enjoy some downtime.

Give kids a choice

When asked when they want to finish their homework, kids might give the first option of "Never" or "Later." But if you ask a few more questions, your kid might tell you what's important to them as they plan their day. This knowledge will enable you to avoid assigning homework during their preferred television show or when they typically play games online with friends.

You will also gain more support from your child when you involve them in decision-making because they will feel that their concerns have been taken into account. Even if you don't agree with them, at least listening to what they have to say will make them feel included. After all, the goal of this homework schedule is for them to finish their assignments.

Allow time for leisure

Some children can enter the house and immediately start working on their homework. They benefit from finishing their work early and having the rest of the evening free to do whatever they want when this occurs. However, most kids need to eat and take a quick break before beginning their assignments. Remember that your child has already spent at least six hours in class as you create a schedule for their homework. Also excluded from this time are travel time to and from school or involvement in extracurricular activities. If your children need some downtime before starting their homework, give them some.

Create a Timeline

Per school grade level, you can typically anticipate 10 minutes of homework. Accordingly, a third-grade student's homework will take them about 30 minutes to finish. The amount of time required, however, can significantly vary between students, teachers, and schools.

Find out how much time the teacher anticipates homework taking each night. Speak with the teacher if your child struggles with their homework or takes a long time to complete it. Your child might require tutoring, additional instruction, or fewer homework assignments.

Pick a Study Location

Establish a convenient location where your children can complete their homework. This workspace needs to be well-lit, well-stocked, and quiet. The workspace should allow you to provide some supervision.

If you have several kids working on their homework at once, you might want to find a different space for each child. While siblings can occasionally be a distraction, kids can sometimes work on their homework at the kitchen table. Decide what's best for your family.

Put everything together

Now that you are aware of your child's needs and concerns regarding finding time to complete homework, you need to create the actual plan. In reality, creating a homework routine is merely a step in creating a daily schedule for the academic year.

Write it down so you can see exactly what they will be doing and when they will be doing it during homework time. For every day of the week, repeat this. Students who are given larger projects must regularly review their homework plans and make any necessary modifications.

You can anticipate consistent effort from your child during the allotted time. A homework session before dinner and another after dinner are not recommended. Children who work intermittently may take longer to get interested in their work than those who work continuously.

Be dependable

Keep to the schedule once you've chosen a time to complete your homework! The majority of kids typically need three weeks to truly establish their new routine.

You might want to carefully consider breaking up the work to take advantage of the time when your child can focus if you notice that your child or teen struggles to focus for the required amount of time while doing their homework.

Children and teenagers who suffer from depression or attention deficit hyperactivity disorder (ADHD) should pay special attention to this additional step. Multiple shorter work sessions and more frequent breaks might be advantageous to them. 1

The following factors

Even though the goal of setting up a homework schedule is to encourage your child to work independently and consistently, you might need to review their finished work. For younger kids, this is especially crucial.

Verify that they comprehended their homework and did a sufficient amount of work during the homework session. Investigate the problem if you notice that your child is struggling to complete their homework during the allotted time. Children occasionally need additional assistance, while other times they just require greater motivation to complete their work.

You might need to look a little further if you discover that your child is still having trouble with their homework despite having a schedule in place. Think about talking to your child's pediatrician or teacher about their problems.

Sometimes unidentified learning disabilities in children cause them to be reluctant to finish their homework. Your child may have a processing disorder or have trouble understanding what they are reading. It's also possible that your child is dealing with a mental health condition like anxiety.

Setting Up Their Own Schedule

Give your child a calendar so they can develop the habit of noting significant dates and occasions. They'll need to remember things like doctor's appointments, play dates, friend birthday parties, games or recitals, and more as they get older. When it comes to knowing what to do and where to be, independent children will rely on themselves rather than their parents.

Learning to Think Independently

Encourage your child to develop their own opinions on everything, from current news events to significant moments in history to made-up stories. Discuss current events over dinner or in the car. Encourage your child to express their opinions to you about various topics. They will know that their opinions matter to you and that their ideas and thoughts are worthwhile and valuable when you truly listen to them.

When you disagree on a topic, it's a great chance for kids to practice respectful debate and speak their minds while also learning to see the good in other people's viewpoints.

Entertaining Themselves

Children need to learn how to identify their interests and how to carve out time for them. Parents can encourage kids to be more independent by, for example, setting up time to read side by side every day, or having kids work on their own activities or just play by themselves while parents finish making dinner. It is acceptable for parents and children to engage in activities independently of one another when you demonstrate to your children that you have your own interests, such as practicing yoga, going for walks with friends, knitting, or catching up on work.

Helping a Child Deal With Uncomfortable Emotions

Kids with strong mental faculties are aware that they can control their emotions rather than letting them control them. Kids who can control their emotions are better able to control their behavior and suppress their negative thoughts. However, children do not naturally understand their emotions or know how to express them in a way that is acceptable in social situations.

Unable to control his anger, a child may act aggressively and have frequent angry outbursts. Similarly, a child who doesn't know what to do when he feels sad may spend hours pouting by himself.

Children who lack emotional literacy may also avoid anything that makes them uncomfortable. For instance, a child who is extremely shy in social settings might shy away from joining a new activity because she doubts her capacity to put up with the discomfort that comes with trying new things.

Many behavioral issues can be solved by teaching children how to control their emotions. A child who is emotionally aware will also be better equipped to handle challenging circumstances and will be more likely to perform at her best. Kids can learn how to deal with their emotions in a healthy way with coaching and practice.

Instill personal accountability

While it's good for kids to feel a range of emotions, it's also crucial for them to understand that they have some control over their emotions. A child can select after-school activities that improve her mood if she had a difficult day at school. A young child who is upset about something her brother did can learn techniques for calming down.

Teach your child about emotions and make sure she understands that strong feelings shouldn't be used as a justification for bad behavior. She has no right to hit someone because she is angry, and feeling sad doesn't have to result in protracted crying.

Teach your child that she is accountable for her own actions and that it is improper to place the blame for her emotions on others. Correct your child's terminology if she hits her brother and says it's because he irked her. Describe how each person is in control of their own thoughts and actions. Her brother might have had an impact on her actions, but he didn't affect her emotionally.

Equally important is teaching your child that she does not control the emotions of other people. It's acceptable if someone becomes upset as a result of her wise choice. To help them resist peer pressure and make wise decisions on their own, children need to learn this lesson time and time again throughout their lives. If you instill strong character and morals in your child, she will have faith in her ability to make wise decisions despite the opinions of others.

You Should Teach Your Child About Feelings

A 4-year-old who doesn't understand why you won't let them have another cookie or an 8-year-old who is upset that you had to leave the playground early because you had to go to work are just two examples of children with whom it can be challenging to deal with feelings.

Since feelings are a fairly abstract concept, teaching them to children can be challenging. It's difficult to put into words how sad, scared, or excited you feel. Since emotions have an impact on every decision a child makes, it's critical to start teaching children about their emotions as early as possible.

Children who are emotionally aware are less likely to express their feelings through tantrums, hostility, or defiance. A kid who knows the phrase "I'm mad at you" is less likely to hit someone. And a kid who knows how to express their hurt feelings is better prepared to settle disputes amicably.

Teach children to incorporate feeling words into their everyday vocabulary. By sharing your emotions when appropriate, you are setting an example for others to follow. "It makes me sad that you don't want to share your toys with your brother today," you can say. He must be depressed as well.

Ask your child how they are feeling each day. If a smiley face chart helps young children choose a feeling, use it. Then, talk about that feeling with them. Discuss the kinds of factors that affect your child's emotions.

Children must learn that they should never hit someone simply because they are angry. Instead, they must develop anger management techniques in order to settle disputes amicably. Actively instruct your child on how to handle unpleasant emotions.

To take a self-timeout. When they become upset, encourage them to go to their room or another peaceful location. Prior to breaking a rule and being placed in timeout, this can help them calm down.

Teach your child constructive coping mechanisms for depressive emotions. Discuss coping mechanisms with your child if they are upset that their friend won't play with them. Kids frequently display aggressive or attention-seeking behaviors when they are sad because they don't know what to do. 1

Develop Your Tolerance for Uncomfortable Emotions

Oftentimes, uncomfortable feelings have a purpose. Anxiety, like being on the precipice of a cliff, is a common emotional reaction designed to warn us of impending danger. However, occasionally we feel fear and anxiety unnecessarily.

Teach your child that just because something makes her anxious doesn't mean it's a bad idea. Encourage her to play soccer, for instance, even if she is reluctant to do so out of concern that she won't get along with the other kids. She will be able to see that she is more capable than she believes if she faces her fears when it is safe to do so.

Sometimes children lose confidence in themselves because they are so accustomed to avoiding discomfort. "I could never do that, it would be too scary," they believe. They lose out on a lot of opportunities as a result.

Encourage your child to venture outside of her comfort zone gently. Give her credit for her efforts and make it clear that you value her willingness to try more than the result. Teach her how to take the opportunity presented by failure, discomfort, and mistakes to learn and improve.

How to Help a Child Change Their Negative Mood

Children's emotions are frequently greatly influenced by their environment. A child might be joyful while having fun and depressed when it's time to go. When she learns she'll be stopping for ice cream on the way home, her attitude might then abruptly change to excitement..

Teach your child that her moods don't always have to be based solely on circumstances outside of her control. Instead, she can exert some control over her emotions despite the circumstances.

Encourage your child to make choices that will lift her spirits. She can take action to make herself feel better so she doesn't become mired in a bad mood, but that doesn't mean she has to suppress or ignore her emotions. Pouting, withdrawing, or complaining for hours on end will only make her feel worse.

Help your child to recognize the decisions she can make to soothe her anger or lift her spirits when she's down. Determine which particular activities will improve her mood. While one child may find that coloring helps them unwind, another might find that playing outside helps them release energy.

When your child is feeling down, point out specific decisions she can make and encourage her to practice attempting to make herself feel better. For instance, if you see her moping, try telling her, "I think moping around today may make you stay stuck in a bad mood. What could you possibly do to improve your mood? Encourage your child to engage in physical activity or try something new to give her the ability to manage her emotions in a healthy way.

Finding constructive ways to pay attention to teenagers can be challenging. Finding family activities they're interested in may be more challenging now that they've outgrown many activities from their younger years.

Teenagers also start to prioritize their time with friends over their time with their families at this time. In addition, many teenagers start to drift away from their parents without a concerted effort to create quality family time.

Even though it's developmentally normal for teenagers to become more independent, it's crucial to put effort into preserving a positive relationship—even when you have communication issues.

Put more emphasis on creating quality time together than on how much time you spend together. Here are ten ways to spend quality time with your adolescent, even if it's only for a short while each day.

1. Switch off all electronics

Face-to-face interaction will probably be hampered in your family by electronics, as it is in the majority of contemporary homes. Set screen time restrictions for the entire family. And establish a household rule dictating when electronics must be turned off.

At least once per week, designate an electronic-free period. Turn off all TVs, computers, and cell phones, even for just an hour, and observe what happens. You'll probably have a lot better success in engaging your teenager in conversation.

2. Share a meal together

Talking to your teen can happen over dinner or at least one other meal each day. Turn off all electronics during mealtimes and concentrate on the conversation. It might be the most effective way to learn about your teen's day.

3. Enter Your Adolescent's World

Your teen probably likes things that you have no idea about. Even if it's not something you particularly enjoy, be willing to enter your teen's world.

If your teen enjoys playing video games, consider playing one together. Allow your teen to explain it to you or show you something.

4. Play a proactive part

On occasion, teenagers dislike sitting and conversing. However, you can have more natural conversations if you play catch with them or engage in some other activity that gets you moving.

5. Collectively perform a kind act for others

Something about performing a kind act significantly enhances a relationship. Making a meal for a neighbor or participating in a community service project can improve your relationship greatly. It can give you time to talk and encourage your adolescent to value doing good deeds.

6. Take a Road Trip Together

Having a conversation in the car can be very effective. You don't have to make eye contact with anyone when you're in a car, which is one benefit. This may make many teenagers feel more at ease discussing sensitive topics.

7. Take a stroll

Going for a walk can be a great way to spend time with your teen while also providing additional health benefits. You can get away from all the distractions at home and have a private conversation by taking a walk around the neighborhood.

8. Work together on a project

Even though many teenagers may object to having to participate in a project, once they get going, they frequently enjoy it. Invite your teen to participate in any activity, such as cleaning your car or painting a room.

9. Introduce New Ideas to Your Teen

Teach your child a brand-new skill. Offer to assist your teen in learning something new, whether it be Chinese language instruction or sharing your culinary expertise.

If your teen is not interested, don't make an effort. However, you will frequently discover that they have a keen interest in knowing how you go about doing things.

10. Plan a family evening

Allocate a certain period of time for family time. Make it a habit, whether it's to watch a movie once a week or play board games once a month. Doing this can help you develop a strong relationship with your adolescent.

1. Sit down and talk about your teen's day.

2. Team up to volunteer.

3. Create a meal together.

4. Together, resolve a challenge. It might be a domestic problem, like how to prevent clutter from piling up on the table, or a larger global issue, like poverty.

5. Attend an outdoor concert.

6. Discuss the horizon. Determine your teen's aspirations for the future and talk to them about what the world might look like in 20, 30, or even 50 years.

7. Discuss the same book after reading it.

8. Take a weekend getaway.

9. Take a hike.

10. see a play.

11. Together, create a new, healthy habit, like working out or keeping a gratitude journal.

12. go to a concert.

13. Discover new cuisines by cooking international dishes or dining at restaurants that serve cuisine you've never tried before.

14. Together, plan a family vacation.

15. Together, develop a monthly menu plan.

16. Take part in a monthly challenge, like walking 30 days straight or saving change for a month.

17. Visit the historic neighborhoods on foot.

18. Attend a ballet.

19. Take a class together, such as one offered locally that teaches graphic design or photography.

20. Attend a neighborhood gathering.

21. Together, create or update a family website or social media page.

22. Do some family tree research.

23. Go to the library.

24. Create a puzzle, then frame it.

25. Create a backyard garden or an indoor container garden.

26. Attend a local author's reading.

27. Make a catch.

28. Have a barbecue.

29. Visit a gallery.

30. Join forces to learn woodworking.

31. learn to make pottery.

32. Stargaze as a group.

33. Together, look for shapes in the clouds.

34. Visit the zoo.

35. Together, study the past of your neighborhood.

36. Construct a time capsule.

37. Observe a parade.

38. Attend a match of a professional sport.

39. Produce a video.

40. Using old blankets and T-shirts, create a pillow.

41. Set up a campfire.

42. Check out a national park.

43. Join one of the yoga classes.

44. Discover a new sport.

45. Co-found a small business.

46. Request a college tour.

47. visit a poetry performance.

48. Order takeout from your teen's preferred fast food restaurant.

49. Spend the day at a lake or the beach.

50. Together, learn how to play a musical instrument.

Teenagers who find it difficult to learn a skill might think they are total failures. A teen who struggles with math, for instance, might conclude they are not intelligent. Or a teenager who doesn't make the soccer team might decide they're not cut out for athletics.

Self-acceptance and self-improvement coexist in a healthy way. Teach your teen that it's possible to accept their faults while also making an effort to improve. Help your teen realize that even though they are having difficulty in school, they can still strive to improve rather than calling themselves "stupid."Help your teen recognize both their strengths and weaknesses to encourage self-improvement. Then, involve them in goal-setting and problem-solving activities so they can work to get better in their weak areas. They should make sure the goals they set are attainable and within their control, and then map out a plan on how they are going to achieve those goals.

Praise Effort Rather Than Outcome: Instead of complimenting your teen on their exam performance, compliment them on all the preparation they undertook. Say, "All that practicing you've been doing has been paying off," as opposed to, "Great job scoring those five points in the game." Show them the value of making a sincere effort and that it's okay if they don't always succeed.

Your teen can control their effort but they can't always control the outcome. In order to prevent them from believing they are only deserving of praise when they succeed, it is crucial to recognize their effort and energy.

Increase Your Self-Assurance

Teenagers need to develop appropriate assertiveness skills. When they don't understand their schoolwork, an assertive teen will be able to ask for assistance rather than letting themselves fall behind.

Speaking up also makes a teen less likely to experience negative peer pressure. When they don't like the way they're being treated, they will speak up for themselves and be able to ask for what they need directly.

Talking about the distinction between assertiveness and aggression will help you teach your adolescent to be assertive. Explain to them that being assertive entails speaking up for oneself in a firm and confident manner without being impolite or yelling at others.

Allowing them to make decisions and reiterating their rights, particularly the right to refuse anything that makes them feel uncomfortable, are two additional ways to instill assertiveness skills in children. By giving them options and allowing them the freedom to refuse things they don't want to do, you can give them plenty of chances to practice being assertive at home.

Encourage Fresh Chances

Teenagers' confidence can increase by taking on challenges, trying new things, and discovering hidden talents. But many teenagers are afraid of failing and don't want to look foolish.

Encourage your teen to take up a new hobby, learn to play an instrument, volunteer, or get a part-time job. They will feel more confident as they gain new skills. Additionally, being a part of a group offers them the chance to make friends and can also boost their self-esteem.

Modeling confidence is important because your teen will pick up the most from your actions rather than your words. If you criticize your appearance or your skills, you'll be modeling that behavior for your child.

Set a good example by demonstrating to others how to take on new challenges with confidence and courage while emphasizing the importance of loving oneself. Discuss with your teen instances in which you showed courage or actions you have taken to boost your self-confidence.

Create Self-Worth

Your teen will struggle to maintain confidence if they only feel good when they receive a certain number of likes on social media or when they can fit into a certain size pair of pants. Low self-esteem eventually results from relying too much on unimportant things, external factors, or other people.

Help your teen develop a strong, positive sense of self-worth. Stress the importance of your principles and teach the lesson that upholding them is a sign of genuine self-worth. Educate them on the value of kindness and compassion over physical attractiveness.

juggling direction and freedom

The idea that you can't trust your adolescent to make wise decisions on their own will only be reinforced if you micromanage their choices. Finding the perfect balance between a lot of direction and enough freedom is crucial.

Give your teen many opportunities to practice the skills you've taught them. If you let them experience natural consequences, they will learn from their mistakes. They'll gradually develop more confidence in their ability to choose wisely.

Encourage others to speak well of themselves

The thoughts that go through your teen's head greatly influence how they feel about themselves. If they are constantly telling themselves, "I'm so ugly," or "No one likes me," they will inevitably feel self-conscious. Help your teen establish a constructive inner dialogue.

Make sure they comprehend how a lot of their beliefs are unfounded and how being too strict can have negative results. In order to stop them from thinking things like "I'm going to fail because I'm stupid," teach them to replace irrational thoughts with more sensible ones, like "I can pass math class if I work hard." Failure-averse teens are less likely to reach their full potential. Because he believes he won't make the team, he might decide against attending the baseball tryouts. Or, he might put off submitting his college application out of concern that he'll receive a rejection letter, which could result in him missing the submission deadline.

Some adolescent people can learn from their mistakes, but some are paralyzed by their irrational fears. The good news is that you can help your adolescent get over his fear of failure so he can heal more quickly. Here are five methods to help your teen get over their fear of failing: Sometimes teenagers make incorrect assumptions about themselves based on their experiences. After failing a math test, a teen may tell himself, "I'm stupid."

On the other hand, a teen who has trouble with baseball might believe that "I can't ever do anything right."

Negative self-talk may reduce your teen's willingness to work harder in the future when faced with challenges.

Encourage your adolescent to use positive self-talk. Encourage him to think realistically instead of pessimistically and to stop talking negatively about himself. If he has a more understanding conversation with himself, he will be better able to bounce back from failure.

Respect your teen's effort more than their results

When given to adolescents, praise for achievement can backfire. You might imply that your love depends on academic success if you say things like, "I'm so proud of you for getting an A on that test," or "I think you're the best trumpet player in the whole band."

No matter the result, compliment your teen on their effort. I'm so glad you spent three hours studying for that science test, you know. It appears to have really paid off. When your teen's attempts are unsuccessful, encourage them by saying things like, "You sure hustled out there on

Talk about failure

Talk with your adolescent about failure. Discuss the negative feelings that result from failure, such as resentment, guilt, shame, and embarrassment. Teach your adolescent how to cope with disappointment.

Mention those who overcame setbacks to achieve success. Make it clear that failing can be a fantastic learning opportunity. Talk about the possible consequences of that attitude and how some people's fear of failing can make them avoid trying things where they might fail.

serve as an illustration of how to deal with failure

Find opportunities to show your teen how to bounce back from setbacks. When you are unable to reach a business agreement or are not hired for a position, set a good example for others. Never pretend to care or justify your behavior.

Discuss your disappointment instead. Then, be sure to explain how you'll use this failure as a learning opportunity so you can move forward and succeed in the future.

Engage in your teen's school life

Participate in your teen's education to foster a supportive environment. You can demonstrate to your child and the teachers that you care about their education by participating in parent-teacher Visiting conferences, dropping by during an open house, and volunteering for the PTA, to name just a few examples. Help your child form positive relationships with teachers. According to studies, when students and teachers get along well, they give it their all in class. Don't criticize your child's teachers in public.

When your teen has problems with a teacher, encourage them to take an active role in problem-solving. Sometimes teenagers make the incorrect assumption that "That teacher doesn't like me" or that "No matter how hard I try in that class, that teacher will always give me a failing grade." Both are true. A teen can position himself for success if he or she can approach the teacher about a grade or request extra assistance when necessary.

"Critical thinking mentality"

Kids face different issues consistently, going from scholarly hardships to issues on the games field. However not many of them have a recipe for tackling those issues. Kids who need critical thinking abilities might try not to make a move when confronted with an issue. As opposed to focusing on tackling the issue, they might concentrate profoundly on keeping away from the issue.2 That's the reason many children fall behind in everyday schedules to keep up with kinships. Different children who need critical thinking abilities get a move on perceiving their decisions. A kid might hit a friend who cuts in line since they don't know what else to do. Or then again, they might leave class when they are being prodded on the grounds that they can't imagine some other ways of making it stop. Those rash decisions might make considerably more pressing issues over the long haul.

The 5 Steps of Problem-Solving

Kids who feel overpowered or miserable frequently won't endeavor to resolve an issue. In any case, when you give them a reasonable recipe for tackling issues, they'll feel more positive about their capacity to attempt. Here are the moves toward issue solving:4

Recognize the issue. Simply expressing the issue without holding back can significantly impact kids who are feeling stuck. Assist your kid with expressing the issue, for example, "You don't have anybody to play with at break," or "You don't know whether you ought to take the high level numerical class."

Foster no less than five potential arrangements. Conceptualize potential ways of taking care of the issue. Underscore that every one of the arrangements don't be guaranteed to be smart thoughts (basically not as of now). Assist your youngster with creating arrangements assuming they are battling to concoct thoughts. Indeed, even a senseless response or implausible thought is a potential arrangement. The key is to assist them with seeing that with just the right amount of innovativeness, they can track down various likely arrangements.

Recognize the upsides and downsides of every arrangement. Assist your kid with recognizing likely sure and unfortunate results for every potential arrangement they distinguished.

Pick an answer. When your kid has assessed the conceivable positive and adverse results, urge them to pick an answer.

Test it out. Advise them to attempt an answer and see what occurs. On the off chance that it doesn't end up actually working, they can continuously attempt one more arrangement from the rundown that they created in sync two.

Work on Solving Problems

When issues emerge, don't race to take care of your youngster's concerns for them. All things considered, assist them with walking through the critical thinking steps. 5 Offer direction when they need help, but do not urge them to tackle issues all alone. On the off chance that they can't concoct an answer, step in and assist them with considering some. 6 But don't naturally guide them.

When you experience conduct issues, utilize a critical thinking approach. 6 Sit down together and say, "You've been experiencing issues finishing your schoolwork of late. We should tackle this issue together." You could in any case have to offer a ramification for bad conduct, yet clarify that you're putting resources into searching for an answer so they can improve sometime later.

Utilize a critical thinking approach to deal with assistance and watch your youngster become more free.

On the off chance that they neglected to pack their soccer spikes for training, inquire, "How might we ensure this doesn't reoccur?" Let them attempt to foster a few arrangements all alone.

Kids frequently foster clever fixes. So they could say, "I'll compose a note and stick it on my entryway so I'll make sure to pack them before I leave," or "I'll gather my sack the prior night and I'll keep an agenda to remind me what necessities to go in my pack."

Give a lot of praise when your youngster rehearses their critical thinking abilities.

Consider Natural Consequences

Regular results may likewise show critical thinking abilities. So when it's fitting, permit your youngster to confront the regular results of their actions. 7 Just ensure it's protected to do as such.

　　　　　

For instance, let your young person burn through all of their cash during the initial 10 minutes you're at a carnival, assuming that is what they need. Then, let them go until the end of the day with practically no burn through cash.

This can prompt a conversation about critical thinking to assist them with settling on a superior decision sometime later. Consider these normal results as a workable second to assist with taking care of together on critical thinking.

Mental Growth

Did you have at least some idea that knowledge isn't permanently established? You might have been raised to accept that certain individuals were only great at testing subjects, and others simply didn't have the inherent capacity to figure out how to settle exceptionally complex math and science issues. You may be astonished to figure out that schooling and cerebrum research in late many years has shown in any case. Specialists have found that kids and grown-ups can create and prepare for intelligence.1 One of the significant variables for having the option to foster this insight is the conviction that knowledge is the consequence of difficult work and study.

Instructors call this a development outlook. The term was instituted by Stanford instructive scientist Dr. Ditty Dweck. Dweck looks at her development mentality to a proper outlook. While individuals with a development mentality accept that they can foster their insight, individuals with fixed outlooks accept that knowledge can't be created. Basically, scientists currently trust that the capacity to gain troublesome and testing material comes from a conviction that you can.2

How Do You Develop a Growth Mindset in Your Children?

These tips are undeniably composed in view of finishing school and schoolwork. You will likely be notified that these are truly moves toward that work for taking care of any issue throughout everyday life. It's great to apply a development mentality to something beyond school work. You maintain that a development outlook should turn into a general demeanor, not restricted to homework.

1. Show Your Children It's Okay to Be Wrong

You know how hard it very well may be to take a stab at something new when you fear falling flat. Showing your kid that it is OK to commit errors will let loose your youngster to attempt another test. During the time spent putting forth that attempt, they will realize what works — and what doesn't.

2. Help Them to Try Out New Ideas and Approaches to Problem Solving

Different issues and undertakings require various methodologies and strategies to be finished. Assuming your kid is battling with an issue, inquire as to whether there is another way that could attempt to take care of the issue.

Despite the fact that you will be enticed to tackle the issue for them, don't. Assuming your kid is truly stuck with an issue, assist them with conceptualizing what else they can attempt to tackle their concern or complete their work. Take a stab at asking them what different assets they have that they can check for more data, like better places in their course book, online sites, or in any event, asking their companions how they tackled an issue.

3. Help Them to Keep Trying to Solve a Hard Problem, Even on the off chance that They Can't See the End Solution

A few issues require a few stages to be finished. You most likely recollect your high level secondary school math classes as having these sorts of issues. However, the new thorough guidelines being utilized in school are intended to open children to issues that should be examined and thoroughly considered — not simply replied through repetition retention or speedy computations.

Work intended to support these critical thinking abilities is being given out in the early grades, to give kids a promising beginning in critical thinking. Instead of advising your youngster to surrender immediately and request the instructor what to do when they see them, have your kid simply start to attempt to deal with it. Some of the time the following stages become clear after the initial steps are taken. Once in a while your kid will understand that they need to distinctively move toward the issue. Indeed, they can't arrive without making those initial not many strides.

4. Show Them the Mantra, "Slip-ups Help My Brain Grow"

Dr. Song Dweck over and over urges educators to remind understudies that missteps assist their cerebrum with developing. She instructs that when somebody effectively finds a response, they have shown the information they as of now have without getting the hang of anything. At the point when somebody commits an error, they are compelled to figure out why and afterward discover some new information simultaneously

Utilizing the expression "Errors Make My Brian Grow" not just removes a portion of the feeling of dread toward conceivably being incorrect, it approves the work expected in committing an error.

It then goes considerably further into empowering realizing what the right response is. Instead of remunerating somebody for being shrewd (fixed mentality), it empowers a way of ceaseless learning.

5. Train Them to Pay Attention to Their Approaches to Problem-Solving

This isn't simply ensuring they are following a progression of moves toward completing their English paper or playing out a numerical calculation. This is requesting that they take a gander at how they, at the end of the day, decided to tackle an issue. Did they attract an image to acquire a superior comprehension of what they are attempting to tackle? Did they search for the particular inquiries they were being posed to by a task?

Critical thinking methodologies can frequently be utilized in different circumstances that may not seem related on a superficial level. You can ask your kid how they chose to tackle an issue or recognize them for halting to contemplate which way to deal with to take care of an issue. You can get some information about this when they finish work assuming that you are sitting close to them while they are working, or when you investigate their work to check whether it is finished.

6. Help Them to Talk About Mistakes

This one isn't tied in with seeming modest. You believe your kid should feel open to talking about what didn't work, so they figure out how to examine ways to deal with tackling issues and finishing work. This can assist them with figuring out how to distinguish what they have previously evaluated that hasn't worked, so they can attempt once more and find what takes care of business. This will likewise assist with growing great abilities for working with others, an expertise acquired in esteem in the working environment.

Being intellectually sound during adolescence entails achieving formative and deep achievements as well as developing robust interaction abilities and the ability to adapt when problems arise. Intellectually strong children experience positive personal fulfillment and can operate successfully at home, school, and in their networks.

Children's mental diseases are characterized as major changes in the way they commonly learn, act, or handle their emotions, resulting in discomfort and difficulty throughout the day. Many youngsters experience occasional anxiety and stress, as well as harmful behaviors. If the negative consequences are significant and long-lasting, interfering with school, home, or play activities, the child may be diagnosed with a psychological condition.

It is simple for guardians to distinguish their kid's actual necessities: nutritious food, comfortable garments when it's chilly, and sleep time at a sensible hour. In any event, a child's psychological and social requirements may not be as obvious. Excellent emotional health allows children to think clearly, grow socially, and learn new skills. Furthermore, old friends and inspiring remarks from adults are really important for supporting children in developing fearlessness, high confidence, and a firm close to home point of view.

A Child's Physical And Mental Health Are Both Important.

Nuts and bolts for a youngster's decent actual wellbeing:

1. Nutritious food

2. Satisfactory safe house and rest

3. Work out

4. Vaccinations

5. Solid living climate

Nuts and bolts for a youngster's decent emotional well-being:

1. Genuine love from family

2. Fearlessness and high confidence

3. The potential chance to play with different kids

4. Empowering educators and steady overseers

5. Completely safe environmental elements

6. Fitting direction and discipline

7. Give youngsters genuine love.

Love, security, and acceptance should be central to daily existence. Children must understand that your love is not contingent on their accomplishments. Mistakes and further losses should be expected and recognized. Certainty reigns supreme in a home filled with boundless love and affection.

Maintain the certainty and confidence of children. congratulate them - Encouraging children's first steps or their ability to become acquainted with another game helps them develop a desire to investigate and learn about their surroundings. Allow children to investigate and play in a safe area where they will not be injured. Grinning and speaking with them constantly will ensure them. Participate in their workouts as a functioning member. Your consideration contributes to their boldness and confidence.

Realistic Goals - Young children require reasonable goals that match their desires with their abilities. With your support, older children can select activities that challenge their abilities and boost their self-esteem.

Be Open - Do not hide your disappointments from your children. They should understand that we all make mistakes. It is really reassuring to learn that adults are fallible.

Avoid Sarcastic Remarks - If a child loses a game or fails an exam, find out how the individual feels about the situation. Children may become discouraged and want a motivational speech. When they are ready, they will chat and reaffirm their proposition.

Encourage children - to make a concerted effort while also taking part in the process. Trying new exercises demonstrates to children collaboration, confidence, and new abilities.

Set aside some time for play!

Encourage Kids to Play

Play is simply enjoyable for children. Nonetheless, recess is as important to their development as food and loving attention. Recess helps children be inventive, develop critical thinking skills, and grasp judgment. Great, vigorous play, which includes running and yelling, isn't simply for fun; it also helps children become truly and intellectually sound.

Children Require Playmates

Occasionally, children get the opportunity with their friends. By playing with others, children discover their strengths and weaknesses, develop a sense of belonging, and learn how to coexist with others. Consider locating a good kids' program through your neighbors, neighboring public venues, schools, or your local park and recreation department.

Guardians Can Make Excellent Playmates

Join in on the fun! Playing Monopoly or coloring with a child is an excellent opportunity to share ideas and hang out in a relaxed setting.

Play for Pleasure

Being involved and sharing in the action is more important than winning. One of the most important questions to ask children is, "Did you have a good time?" rather than, "Did you win?" We typically recognize just achievement and winning in our goal-oriented society. This attitude can be discouraging and discouraging to children who are learning and experimenting with new exercises. Children should take an interest and enjoy it.

Television viewing should be monitored

Make an attempt not to use TV as a "sitter" on a regular basis. Choose TV shows for children with care. A few shows can be both educational and entertaining.

School should be enjoyable

For children, starting school is a momentous time. "Playing school" can be a beneficial way to give kids a taste of school life.

Enroll them in a pre-school, Head Start, or comparable neighborhood program that gives them the opportunity to interact with other children and establish new friends. Children can learn academic principles as well as how to simply determine and adjust to problems.

Provide sufficient guidance and educational discipline

Children require the opportunity to explore and develop new abilities and freedom. Simultaneously, children must learn that certain behaviors are unacceptable and that they are accountable for the repercussions of their actions.

Children, as members of a family, must become acquainted with the rules of the nuclear family. Provide fair and consistent direction and discipline. They will apply these interaction abilities and rules to school and, eventually, the workplace.

Discipline and Guidance Concepts

With your assumptions, be strong yet compassionate and reasonable. The development of your children is dependent on your love and comfort.

Set a true model. You can't expect discipline and self-control from a child if you don't practice this manner of behaving.

Criticize the behavior, not the child. It is preferable to remark, "That was something dreadful you did," rather than "You are a nasty kid or young lady."

Abstain from irritating, dangers and bribery.Children will figure out how to overlook pestering, and dangers and pay-offs are only sometimes powerful.

Give kids the reasons "why" you are restraining them and what the likely outcomes of their activities may be.

Discuss your sentiments. We as a whole blow our top every once in a while. Assuming you do "go insane," it is critical to discuss what occurred and why you are irate. Apologize assuming that you were off-base!

Keep in mind, the objective isn't to control the kid, however for that person to learn poise.

Give a completely safe home

It's acceptable for youngsters to feel apprehensive now and then. Everybody fears something sooner or later in their life. Dread and nervousness outgrow encounters that we don't have any idea.

On the off chance that your kids have fears that won't disappear and influence their way of behaving, the initial step is to figure out the thing is terrifying them. Be adoring, patient and consoling, not basic. Keep in mind: the apprehension might be genuine to the youngster.

Indications Of Fear

Apprehensive quirks, modesty, withdrawal and forceful way of behaving might be indications of young life fears. An adjustment of ordinary eating and resting examples may likewise flag an unfortunate trepidation. Kids who "play wiped out" or feel restless routinely may have a few issues that need consideration.

Apprehension about school can happen following an unpleasant occasion, for example, moving to another area, evolving schools, or after a terrible episode at school.

Children should not return to school after being home sick for an extended period of time.

When to Seek Assistance

Guardians and relatives are usually fast to notice if a child strongly hates feelings or behavior. Your observations, together with those of teachers and other guardians, may drive you to seek treatment for your child. If you suspect a problem or have questions, consult your pediatrician or a psychological health expert.

Cautioning Signs

1. The accompanying signs might demonstrate the requirement for proficient help or assessment

2. Decrease in school execution

3. Less than stellar scores in areas of strength for notwithstanding

4. Customary concern or tension

5. Rehashed refusal to go to the everyday schedule part in typical kids' exercises

6. Hyperactivity or squirming

7. Steady bad dreams

8. Constant defiance or animosity

9. Successive fits

10. Misery, bitterness or crabbiness

11. Get familiar with explicit psychological wellness conditions and youngsters

12. ADHD - attentional issues

13. Bipolar Disorder - discouragement and high energy

14. Lead Disorder - social issues

15. Discouragement - pity

16. Sadness - adapting to misfortune

17. Psychosis - hearing voices or seeing things that aren't there

18. Self destruction - considerations of death/biting the dust

19. Substance use - drinking and utilizing drugs

20. Where to look for help

Data and references in regards to the sorts of administrations that are accessible for kids might be acquired from:

1. Emotional wellness associations, hotlines and libraries

2. Different experts like the youngster's pediatrician or school advisor

3. Different families locally

4. Family network associations

5. Local area based mental consideration

6. Emergency outreach groups

7. Training or custom curriculum administrations

8. Family asset focuses and support gatherings

9. Wellbeing administrations

10. Insurance and backing for gatherings and associations

11. Self improvement and care groups

Being intellectually sound during adolescence entails achieving formative and close-to-home accomplishments, as well as learning sound interactive abilities and how to adapt when problems arise. Intellectually strong children have a positive sense of self-worth and can function effectively at home, school, and in their networks.

Analyzing Your Communication with Your Child

We frequently find it challenging to look at our own actions with objectivity. Imagine that you are recording your interactions with your child and listening to the audio and video as you think about how you would describe your daily interactions with your child. Would you sound kind and patient in voice?

How attentive and interested did you seem to be to your child's speech? Or would you prefer to check your phone for messages or send texts to friends rather than giving your child your full attention? In other words, would you believe you were at your best if you recorded and then played back a recording of yourself?

If the response is no, consider what you can do to modify the way you speak with your child. When you're telling your child what she did wrong, is your tone harsh, impatient, or angry? If your child didn't do anything wrong, do you still sound angry with her because you're worn out?

Even if you're correcting a behavior issue, be mindful of your tone of voice and how you can soften it when you speak to your child.

The Benefits of Using a Positive Tone

Here are some key explanations for how your voice tone and the words you use can greatly improve the interactions and communication between parents and their children.

You Can Expect Your Child to Listen more

This is common sense. Which would you prefer—a person speaking to you in a stern or critical manner or someone speaking to you in a nice, calm manner? A gentle voice, even if it is firm, will probably get more of your child's attention and encourage her to listen to what you have to say, even if there is a disagreement or you need to correct something your child is doing.

Being strict is ineffective

When you yell at your child or use aggressive language, you're less likely to succeed and could even sour your relationship. In fact, research indicates that screaming can be just as harmful as strict discipline. Speaking nicely is undoubtedly the better option if you want your child to acquire the skills necessary to control his own behavior. Sure, your child may listen in the short term.

Children pick up on our behaviors

Speaking politely to your child will make her more likely to do the same for you. And if you speak negatively and harshly to her all the time? You can probably guess what you'll get out of that.

Your relationship will be stronger

You'll strengthen your relationship with your child if you show them respect and kindness. When speaking to your child, use the words "Thank you" and "please," and make it clear that you expect him to use these words in return. You will become closer if you treat one another with respect and courtesy; on the other hand, mean words and a harsh voice will make you distance yourself.

Your Youngster Will Show More Respect

When you speak to your child in a pleasant tone at home, she will naturally do so at school and in other situations. Soon, people around your child will remark on how well-mannered and polite she is, and she'll be proud of these abilities, which will serve her well as she enters adolescence and beyond.

Imagine a respectful, well-mannered teen who knows how to communicate! When you begin to instill these skills now, it is possible.

Your remarks are excessive

When speaking with children, the best course of action is to keep your remarks brief and limited to one or two points. It can be challenging for a child to remember everything that is expected of them when you give them a list of things to remember, such as a list of several chores you want them to complete or a reminder to complete a number of tasks in order to get ready for school.

Similar to this, using many big words and giving a lengthy justification for something, like the reason you punished her for doing something wrong, can only serve to muddle the message.

With younger children's short attention spans comes the need to be succinct and specific.

Your kid is preoccupied with something else

Frequently, kids are focused on what they're doing so intently that they simply don't hear you, whether it's watching a favorite show or movie or playing with Legos. Kids can become completely absorbed in something just like adults can, so when they don't listen sometimes it's not so much defiance as it is that they are totally absorbed in something.

Try to look at this positively—they are improving their ability to focus— and ask your child for her full attention by approaching her and speaking to her directly.

Allow your child some time to move from the activity she is engaged in to the task you have for her.

They Are Performing Other Activities

You yell at your child from across the room or from another part of the house because you are busy making dinner and want to remind him to finish his homework. But whenever you can, try to establish the habit of going to him and having a face-to-face conversation with him. If you fully focus on your child when making a request, your chances of getting him to listen to you are greatly increased.

You're placing an order or pleading

Going full drill sergeant ("Pick up those toys right now!!!") or pleading beggar ("Please, please, please, can't you pick up your toys?") is likely to end up with the same outcome over time—children who don't listen.

Make demands in a polite but firm manner. Find the right balance with your child between giving orders and pleading.

You Vary Your Position

You are teaching your child to ignore you if you ask him to pick up his toys over and over again without enforcing consequences when he refuses.

You Make Criticisms

Would you like it if someone was always berating you, and would you want to listen to what they had to say? Your child may unintentionally tune you out if you are consistently critical ("I don't know why you can't ever listen!").

How to Recognize If You're Gaslighting Your Children

How to Make a Child Pay Attention

How do you get a child to pay attention to what you are saying now that you are aware of some potential reasons why he or she might not listen? Consider using some of these methods to develop your listening abilities.

We understand one another. Ask your child to look at you directly while you are speaking to each other by getting down on his level. This is a great way to not only ensure that your child is paying attention, but also to teach him good manners and how to listen politely when someone is speaking to him.

Take your child's advice into consideration. Like other skills, your child will pick up listening skills by imitating your behavior. If you train your child to expect you to listen to her when she speaks, she will be more likely to reciprocate when you speak to her.

Identify the cause of their noncompliance. Consider any potential reasons why your child may not be listening to you. Are you requesting of him something that he cannot handle on his own? Is he grumpy or exhausted and finding it difficult to do what you ask? Instead of dismissing it as your child being disrespectful, deliberately being defiant, or ignoring you, think about what might be causing his behavior.

Maintain composure. Even though it may be frustrating when your child refuses to listen, try to maintain your composure and zen while guiding them. Also, try to avoid yelling or speaking angrily. Why? two main factors One, when you lose control and become angry, you are teaching your child that she has the power to make you angry. And two, shouting might work in the short run, but it will eventually lose its effectiveness.

Describe why it is disrespectful. Teach your child that it's not polite to ignore or not pay attention to someone who is speaking to you..

Inject a little fun. If you frequently struggle to get your children to pay attention, try changing the dynamic of your interactions by being a little more playful. Using timers to compete in a race to the door or setting up a sticker chart to reward him with something he wants if he can get ready on time for a week or more are two strategies you can use if you are frustrated with your child's tardiness and inability to get ready for school on time. Instead of demanding something from him, use your imagination to encourage cooperation.

Flip the script. In order for your child to understand that you aren't actually ignoring her, be sure to let her know in advance that you'll be doing this exercise: Tell your child that you won't be listening to her for the next 30 minutes (or more or less depending on your child's age and how she responds). Your child won't need much time to realize how awful it is to have someone you want to talk to ignore you.

Be tolerant. The process of developing effective communication habits can take a long time. Instead of expecting your child to always comply with you the moment you command it, consider his growing ability to listen as a crucial component of laying the groundwork for a solid relationship between the two of you in the years to come.

Regular meals with children have been linked to an increased likelihood of positive developmental outcomes like better health and eating habits, strong mental, emotional, and social skills, improved behavior, and better academic performance, according to an impressive body of research.

Schedule family dinners whenever you can, as much as you can, even if you are unable to do so every night. Even if your weeknights are jam-packed with extracurricular activities or late hours at work, there are still ways to make it work, like eating breakfast or snacks together. The key is to make family meals fun, talk about the day, and stay connected with your kids.

Similar to dinnertime, bedtime is a great time to talk to your children about their days. You can pose questions to them like, "What was the best part of your day today?" or "What was the funniest thing that happened today?" that will compel them to provide detailed responses.

Then, be sure to discuss your day in detail, including any accomplishments you were most proud of, any problems you may have, and your strategy for resolving them. You can demonstrate to your child how much you value them as a person and how close you feel to them by telling them something personal about yourself. Additionally, you deepen your relationship and let them know how much they mean to you.

By having fun together, you can strengthen your relationship with your children. Ride bikes outside or kick a soccer ball around with your friends. Or, choose a fun family board game (make it educational if you want to find something that will mentally challenge them) and encourage them to practice good manners and great social skills, like learning how to be a gracious winner or loser, while you are all having a good time.

The fact that you're having fun together is more important than the activity itself. You can watch a great children's film and then "review" it, as well as create entertaining crafts, prepare meals you both love, bake treats, and more. Do something you both like and connect to while doing it, just like you would with a partner. Kids can be annoying at times and undoubtedly make mistakes. However, parents must remember that treating children with respect is just as significant as correcting them when necessary. You can talk to your child in a loving and calm manner even if they have done something that calls for discipline.

It has been demonstrated that yelling or using physical punishment is not only ineffective but can also degrade the quality of your relationship with your child.

You should not reserve the use of good manners for social situations outside the home. Children should be reminded to say "please" and "thank you," and you should follow suit!

Your relationship will improve and your home will be a more enjoyable place to live if you treat one another with respect and consideration.

your spouse or a good friend

Giving children chores and responsibilities helps them feel valued and builds their self-confidence because kids naturally love to help.

Tell them how impressed you are with their work and how much you value their assistance. It will not only strengthen your bond but also assist your children in developing into self-assured, charitable, and compassionate adults.

In addition to being a wonderful way to bond with your child and strengthen your parent-child relationship, research indicates that hugging and cuddling may also lower your risk of becoming ill. Therefore, show your child your love by giving her many hugs throughout the day, and she will grow up hugging you in return!

Write a note and place it in your child's lunchbox as one way to show your child you care about them every day. Planning enjoyable activities for the weekends and listening intently to your child when they speak can both significantly improve the quality of your relationship with them.

Showing your child how much you value him on a daily basis will help to fortify your relationship with him and make it enduring and unbreakable.

Children frequently seem hard-wired to push boundaries and test them. This can occasionally mean that parents make numerous attempts in vain to teach their children to respect them and learn to make wiser decisions in the future. Children don't seem to listen, and they frequently disregard warnings of impending disciplinary measures, so it's understandable why parents become discouraged and frustrated.

Have a well-thought-out plan for what to do when the law is broken to combat this. The issue is frequently that punishments are not applied in the most efficient manner to prevent misbehavior and teach expectations. The good news is that changing just a few small aspects of your discipline methods can have a significant impact on children's behavior.

When given and enforced properly, consequences can alert your child to the fact that you're serious about taking control of the situation. However, try to implement them in a loving, firm manner that emphasizes rewarding positive behavior rather than punishing inappropriate behavior.

The goal of using consequences is not to humiliate, embarrass, shame, or make your child feel unloved. Instead, this strategy ought to jog their memories of the fact that misbehavior can lead to unpleasant outcomes (like losing their electronics).

Both positive and negative effects require consistent application to be effective. They won't learn to stop hitting their siblings if you only take away their video games two out of every three times they do it.

The message that you're not really serious about what you say and/ or that you can be persuaded to change your mind is conveyed by the inconsistent imposition of consequences. The best strategy is to punish kids for breaking the rules every single time they do it. You can also assign favorable repercussions to the behaviors you want to see more of.

You must be consistent if you want to teach your kids that misbehavior will not be tolerated.

Consequences must also be followed precisely. Never cave before you've revoked a privilege for the day. Make a commitment to yourself that you will always say what you mean and act on it. Your child might take some time to comprehend and come to trust that you will keep your word, but if you are persistent, they will change their minds. Then there's a good chance that your kids' behavior will change and they'll start paying attention to you again.

Concentrate on the good

Having a good, loving relationship with your children will help you discipline them effectively. Consequences will be much more effective if your children respect you. As a result, make an effort to show your children affection for at least 15 minutes each day.

As you spend more time with your children, they will spend less time in time out.

Take your child for a stroll during this time, or pay close attention to what they are saying when they speak. Talk about shared memories while looking through some old pictures. Together, read a favorite book. Complete a simple baking task.

Their moment has come, and that is the main idea. Try to give them your undivided attention. Don't check your phone when you think no one is looking, so don't do it. **Increase the amount of time you spend with your kids.**

Describe the Impact Clearly

Use time-sensitive consequences whenever possible. You're grounded until I say otherwise, is not a clear enough statement. Both are not saying, "You can't leave until I can trust you again."

Giving consequences with an ambiguous end date could indicate that you aren't being sincere and are instead making a hasty threat. Additionally, your child might learn that everything will end soon. Or else, your kid might think you're being overly strict in your response. They have little motivation to start acting in accordance if they believe they will never be able to win your favor again.

Always specify the duration of the consequence. It's usually acceptable to take something away from children for 24 hours.

Say something like, "Until this time tomorrow, you've lost your electronics." On occasion, you might want to deny your children a privilege until they earn it back. In this instance, the penalties are in place to encourage good behavior, such as completing homework assignments on time or maintaining a tidy bedroom.

If this is the case, make sure your children understand exactly what needs to happen for them to earn back what was taken from them. This makes it clear what conduct is expected of them and maintains a neutral environment rather than one that is hostile or overtly hostile. The relationship between your child's behavior and the consequence is also emphasized by this method.

Connecting Action to Effects

Say, "You can earn your phone back for an hour each night when your homework is finished," as opposed to, "You can't have your phone back until I can trust you."

Give Repercussions Right Away

The best outcomes happen right away. It is unlikely that taking away your kids' planned visit with Grandma the following week will have the same impact as taking away their electronics today.

Children are more likely to remember the reasons they got into trouble if there are swift consequences. They are more likely to forget the rule they broke if it is delayed by a week. Additionally, experiencing the repercussions immediately after misbehaving can inspire people to refrain from repeating it.

It might occasionally be impossible to provide immediate consequences, though. The punishment will obviously be postponed if you learn that your kids were in trouble on the bus three days ago. Alternatively, if they act inappropriately right before leaving for school in the morning, you might need to wait until they get home before defining and enforcing a consequence.

When the punishment cannot be applied immediately, inform your children as soon as you can. Remind them of the rule they broke so they understand why they are now in trouble.

Consequence-Based Education

Consequences and punishments are not the same thing. The use of consequences as a teaching tool is recommended. They are not meant to humiliate children the way punishments frequently do. Punishments frequently worsen behavioral issues rather than improve them.

Instead, logical outcomes promote better behavior by ensuring that the punishment is appropriate for the offense. So, if your children won't put their video games away, take them away. Alternately, if they ride their bike outside the allowed areas, take the bike away.

A poor grade follows naturally if your older child fails an exam at school due to lack of preparation. Another option is to impose a logical punishment, such as denying access to video games, adding extra chores, or skipping out on social events.

You might even want to involve older children and teenagers in brainstorming potential punishments for different transgressions. They might be even more critical of themselves than you are, and they might be more tolerant of the repercussions if they have a say in what they will be.

Adjust It to the Age

Developing consequences for your kids based on their developmental stage is crucial for effective discipline, according to experts. For instance, if a young child disobeys a rule, you might decide to remind them that doing so will result in a time out. With young children, the mere mention of the punishment is frequently sufficient to alter behavior.

Naturally, you'll need to be ready to act decisively if they refuse. Simply remove your child from the situation for a set amount of time if the rule is broken again. (One minute for every year of age is suitable.) For kids ages 3 and up, you may decide to let them orchestrate their own time-out. Say, "You will need to go to time-out now, but you can come back when you feel ready and you are in control." This promotes self-management skills and helps your child learn self-control. And it can work quite well with older kids and teens, too.

Switch It Up

When used too frequently or for too many different purposes at once, consequences may lose some of their effectiveness. Children who lose privileges repeatedly over a long period of time may lose interest in working to earn them back. A time-out, for instance, tends to lose some of its effectiveness if it is used repeatedly throughout the day.

Or the punishment you are applying might not be the best one to bring about the desired changes. Maybe restricting a different privilege would be more effective if your usual tactic is to eliminate screen time.

Every child occasionally sins, disobeys the law, and pushes the boundaries. Setting limits and providing effective discipline are the responsibility of parents in order to deter bad behavior and reward good. Parents are aware of this, but it is frequently easier said than done. In fact, almost every parent will acknowledge that determining the best course of action can be very difficult, especially when the situation is tense.

Children learn to make better decisions in the future when adults react in a collected, supportive, and consistent manner. Adult interventions, however, are not all created equal, and some could even be harmful.

There is a significant distinction between imposing consequences on children and menacing punishments. The latter frequently encourages more harmful behavior and may harm a child's self-esteem as well as the relationship between parents and children. Instead, parenting experts recommend the discipline tactic of implementing consequences as an effective way to curb future transgressions.

Differences between Punishment and Consequence

Both consequences and punishments aim to mold and control children's behavior, but their effects on children differ significantly. To make children suffer or feel guilty for their transgressions is the goal of punishments. They may be done intentionally to hurt children. The objective is for the child to connect their behavior with the results of their actions and gain the necessary comprehension and motivation to make a different choice the next time, even though consequences may cause some discomfort.

Illustrations of Penalties

Punishments can include yelling, criticizing, humiliating, threatening, taking away privileges, and physical harm (also known as corporal punishment). They are frequently not directly related to the child's behavior. For instance, if a parent asks a 5-year-old to pick up their toys, the child may receive a spanking. The physical discomfort is meant to serve as a constant reminder to the child to never repeat the behavior. According to research, the child might only experience fear, rage, or resentment as a result of being hit.

Other instances include giving a child an embarrassing haircut to "teach them a lesson" after they misbehaved at school or washing out their mouth with soap after they talked back. Another punishment could involve taking pictures and posting them on social media to publicly shame a tween for not keeping their room tidy. Or intentionally running over a 14-year-old's baseball glove in the driveway with the car.

Consequences aim to teach kids how to behave better in the future rather than to punish a child for making a mistake. They are produced by adults and are a direct result of inappropriate behavior.

For instance, parents might take away a 5-year-old's toys for the rest of the day if they don't pick up after themselves when instructed to. A 7-year-old may be given an additional task to complete if they argue with their parents. Parents may take away a 9-year-old's electronics for the evening if they misbehave at school. A 12-year-old may not be permitted to use their phone until their bedroom is clean if they don't clean it.

The above examples are logical consequences that a parent puts in place in response to a child's misbehavior. Another effective type of consequence to impose is natural consequences. These require the parent to simply allow the results of the child's actions to occur. Natural consequences are a direct result of a child's behaviors. Adults may allow kids to face the natural consequences of their choices when it's safe to do so and when a child is likely to learn an important life lesson.

For instance, if a student forgets to pack a coat, they risk getting cold at recess. They might perform poorly if they don't prepare for a test. They might miss their soccer practice if they don't get ready on time. Other instances of natural consequences include the fact that an 8-year-old will become hungry later if they refuse to stop playing so they can eat lunch. A 10-year-old risks ruining their trading cards if they leave them outside in the rain.

Punishments might be effective in the short run. Children may comply out of fear of you or because they want you to stop hurting or humiliating them. In the long run, however, punishments can backfire, harm the parent-child relationship, and result in low self-esteem. Additionally, they lose their effectiveness because children aren't developing the skills necessary for wise decision-making.

Instead, using logical and natural consequences teaches kids that, even though they made a poor decision, they can still make better ones in the future. In the end, consequences are more effective at addressing children's behavioral issues and turning missteps into teaching moments.

Before your children leave the nest, you can form relationships with them that will last a lifetime. But consistent quality time together is the secret to forging those bonds. The important thing is that you are developing relationships with one another through fulfilling experiences, whether that be playing a board game every night after dinner, organizing regular pizza nights, or volunteering to clean up the park.

Allow your children to participate in decision-making as they get older and to occasionally select their own activities. If you prioritize and safeguard your family time, you will have created a foundation of special moments and memories that will keep you close to your children as they grow older.

Spending time together is one of the greatest gifts families can give to one another. Not only does sharing quality time strengthen and build family bonds, but it also provides a sense of belonging and security for everyone in the family.

Research shows that when families engage in enjoyable activities, children not only gain important social skills but also experience higher self-esteem.Strong family ties also foster better behavior in kids, enhance parent-child communication, improve academic performance, and teach kids how to be good friends.

As a parent, you play a key role in cultivating and protecting these family bonds. However, developing close family ties is not always a natural process. It may require extra effort to find time for your family in our busy daily lives. Commit to these 10 crucial habits if you want your family to have this solid foundation.

Plan family time

Planning is necessary to guarantee that you spend enough quality time with your family, whether you have kids in school or teenagers.

                    10 Minutes To Become A Better Parent

Schedule family time. By looking at everyone's schedule, you can determine whether there are any time slots that can be set aside for family time. Try to choose a regular family activity night, perhaps once a week, when everyone gathers for fun. Everyone will be aware that they must save that night for family time if it is kept on a regular schedule.

Plan excursions. Plan regular day trips as another way to fit family time into your schedule. If your family thinks this would be fun, try to schedule the trip at least one month in advance. Make sure everyone is aware of the plan by posting it on the family calendar.

Make new customs. By picking the first strawberries of the summer or carving pumpkins every Halloween, you can establish family traditions while you are all together. Some families enjoy signing up for the same neighborhood festival each year or participating in a 5K walk or run.

Having Dinner with Others

Pick a few nights each week when you anticipate everyone to be assembled at the dinner table. Don't allow phones or other electronics. Just eat a meal (something easy is fine!) and have a conversation together.

Children's physical and mental health benefit from eating meals together, according to studies. Additionally, it can improve relationships within the family and communication.

If your family's schedules prevent you from eating dinner together, consider having breakfast instead. The important thing is to get together and have a distraction-free meal.

As a family, perform chores

Make maintaining your yard or cleaning your house a family-wide obligation. Ask everyone to sign up for the tasks on a list that has been created. After that, designate a day or time during the week or weekend when everyone can work on their chores simultaneously.

If your teenagers have a busy schedule and require a little extra time, set a deadline for them to complete their chores. However, remind them that working together on a task makes it go much more quickly than working alone.

A sense of teamwork can also be fostered by doing chores together, particularly if someone finishes their chores early and is willing to assist another family member. Plan a small reward for when the work is finished, such as going out for ice cream, watching a movie, or playing a board game, to make doing chores more enjoyable.

Establish a mission statement

Most parents associate mission statements with for-profit companies and non-profit organizations. However, these documents also function well for families. Making a family mission statement can assist you in determining your family's priorities, despite the fact that it might sound a little corny or too businesslike.

A family mission statement can serve as a reminder of your family's guiding principles or the qualities you cherish most in one another. It's a great project for family night because it's easy to put together and enjoyable to do as a family. It's not necessary for your statement to be lengthy or intricate. Simple statements like "In our family, we love each other and support each other" will do (but feel free to let your kids come up with a long list if they want!).

Once finished, place your mission statement prominently on display in your house. Read it, consult it, and discuss it frequently. It aids in establishing what is significant to your family.

Hold family gatherings

Family gatherings are a good opportunity for everyone to check in, voice complaints, or plan the future. For instance, a family gathering is a good opportunity to discuss a future day trip, family vacation, or how you intend to get your chores done the following weekend.

These meetings can be planned as events on your family calendar, or they can be unscheduled, with the option for any family member to call one if they feel the need. Goal-setting for the family can also be done at family gatherings.

Read your family mission statement at the beginning of each of these gatherings. If your family is large, start by asking if anyone has a concern or an agenda item. Write down the topics that each person wants to discuss, then go over each one one at a time.

You might need to establish some ground rules for the meeting, such as allocating a certain amount of time to each item on the agenda and enforcing a "no talking" policy when someone else is speaking.

		

Also emphasize the importance of showing kindness, respect, and consideration. These meetings' objective is to find constructive solutions to family problems.

Encourage and Back up

One of the most crucial components of creating strong family ties is feeling supported by your family. Such connections will bind your children for life.

Encourage everyone to find out what is important to their family members and to try their best to support one another during the good and the bad times in order to foster a sense of community. Everyone in the family should feel free to express both good and bad news and receive a supportive response.

The intention is for the entire family to share in the good times and the bad, and to support one another. Families are much more likely to survive difficult times when they feel supported. 5

10 Simple Ways to Improve Family Cohesion

Plan your time off

Even though spending time with family is a vital part of daily life, everyone also needs downtime. You must set aside time for yourself in addition to encouraging your children to spend some quiet time alone to recharge.

Being a parent is a huge responsibility that can be taxing. So never feel guilty about taking a break. Companies are required by the U.S. Department of Labor to provide employees with breaks throughout the working day. So make sure you are giving yourself some alone time. When you do, you will become a better parent.

Together, we volunteer

Research shows that the more we give, the happier and more appreciative of our own lives we become. Giving your time and effort to better the lives of others is also a powerful learning experience.Additionally, your family's bond will be strengthened if everyone participates in these educational opportunities together.

What's more, volunteering can expose kids to lots of different people and increase their appreciation for those who are different from them. Additionally, it teaches kids to be less egotistical and more empathic.

Volunteering has also been linked to a number of improved health outcomes, including better physical and mental health, increased life satisfaction, higher self-esteem, and decreased depressive symptoms. Encourage your child's pursuits

Strong families encourage the interests of their members. It's important to encourage your child's interests, whether that means going to their soccer games, reading a book series they adore, or lending a hand as they amass action figures from their favorite movies or TV shows.

Give your child some support if they participate in sports, band, Scouts, or any other school activity. If taking on a leadership role is not your style, you are not required to do so. Find a way to let your children know that you appreciate what they are doing and want to help them succeed in whatever they are pursuing.

Ask your children for their opinions if you aren't sure where you can offer assistance. Asking shows that you are interested in the topics they are interested in.

The longest and most significant relationships your children will ever have are probably those they have with one another. However, there will probably be times when you feel more like you are rearing bitter rivals than devoted siblings.

Sibling rivalry is common, though, and conflicts can teach us valuable lessons. Additionally, just because siblings quarrel doesn't preclude their continued closeness..

Whether your siblings are biological, step-siblings, or adopted, there are a number of things you can do to help them become closer.

Studying Sibling Relationships

Siblings play a crucial role in teaching one another how to interact socially.

According to Laurie Kramer, a professor at the University of Illinois who has studied siblings in-depth, parents are better at imparting the social graces of more formal settings, such as how to behave in public and how to avoid embarrassing oneself at the dinner table. However, siblings make better role models for the more informal behaviors that make up the majority of a child's daily experiences, such as how to act in public places like schools and streets or around friends. 2

  10 Minutes To Become A Better Parent

Creating strong relationships between siblings may eventually lead to your children becoming best friends. Siblings will argue and fight, but working out their differences can help them become more mature in their relationships with one another and other people.

They'll be more socially adept

According to research, siblings give children better social skills. Perhaps children who grow up with many siblings and learn how to share, cooperate, and compromise become successful social beings as adults.

They'll Work Better Together

Sibling experience may give children life skills that make them better partners. Children who grow up with siblings are less likely to divorce, according to a 2014 study published in the Journal of Family Issues. In fact, the likelihood of divorce decreases by 3% for every sibling a child has.

According to studies, the quality of sibling relationships is what determines how beneficial they are. Strong sibling relationships help children grow in their social skills.

Relations between tense siblings can become destructive. Adolescent anxiety and depression may be more prevalent in siblings who don't get along with one another.

Providing a Good Example

Sibling relationships that are close can encourage younger siblings to imitate the older ones. Positive feelings between siblings are associated with similar educational achievements. Therefore, an older sibling who attends college may have a positive influence on encouraging younger siblings to do the same.

Unfortunately, younger siblings may also imitate bad decisions. If their older sisters had children when they were teenagers, girls were more likely to do the same. If their older siblings have engaged in risky sexual behavior, teens are also more likely to do the same.

In order to ensure that older children set a positive example for the younger ones, it is crucial to promote healthy relationships. Here are some methods for fostering closer relationships and stronger bonds between your children.

Develop Emotional Control Skills

There is no doubt that sibling relationships are highly emotional, even without a study to support it. Children act in ways toward their siblings that they would never act in ways toward their friends.

There is something about siblings that elicits strong emotions, whether they are yelling at one another, accusing one another of cheating, or arguing over who gets the last cookie. Siblings frequently elicit from one another the emotions of anger, frustration, jealousy, anxiety, and irritability.

Sibling relationships can be challenging for siblings to maintain when these emotions are not managed. Fortunately, research indicates that teaching children to control their emotions can lead to stronger relationships.

Researchers have found that kids who are better at managing their emotions require less parental direction. Prosocial sibling relationships are also encouraged by improved emotion regulation skills.

Your children could benefit from using these techniques to develop better emotional control:

Discuss your feelings. As you speak to your children on a regular basis, incorporate feeling words to help them acquire the vocabulary they need to discuss their emotions. Read books about feelings, pause movies to talk about the emotions of the characters, and identify specific instances when you have felt various emotions.

Write down their feelings. By giving their emotions names in real time, you can assist your children in learning to recognize the emotions they're experiencing. Say things like, "It appears that you are currently feeling angry." Is that accurate? or "I understand you feel scared about this."

Differentiate between emotions and behavior. Make it clear that while having feelings is always acceptable, everyone has a choice in how they express them. Therefore, while being angry is acceptable, hitting is not.

Determine effective coping mechanisms. Teach your kids healthy ways to deal with their feelings. Taking a few deep breaths or leaving a heated argument are better ways to control anger than losing your temper..

Give consequences as needed. Give your kids a consequence if they violate the rules out of emotion. The best ways to help kids learn from their errors so they can be kinder to their siblings in the future might be time-out, loss of a privilege, or restitution.

Show No Favoritism

It may be hard to resist favoring one of your children. It makes sense that you would identify more with one or would frequently give that person the benefit of the doubt than with the others.

Furthermore, it can be tempting to single out the best-behaving person, saying things like, "Well, if you all behaved more like your brother, we could do more fun things together."

But choosing a favorite doesn't benefit anyone. According to studies, sibling conflict is exacerbated when favoritism is perceived. Even after you stop picking favorites, it may have a long-lasting impact that prevents them from becoming close friends as adults. According to research, memories of favoritism as a child make it difficult for siblings to remain close as adults.

Giving one child special privileges or extending more warmth and affection to them simply because they relieve your stress is an example of harmful favoritism.

Sayings like, "But your sister can clean her room before dinner," should be avoided. How come not? or "When your brother was your age, I never had to remind him to do his homework." Children will become more resentful and angry as a result of these kinds of remarks.

Fairness should not be confused with favoritism, though. It's acceptable for kids to occasionally believe that things are unfair. Everyone need not be treated equally.

Children should earn privileges in accordance with their level of maturity, and your parenting techniques should be compatible with the way your child learns. Even though kids may occasionally object that an older sibling gets to stay up later, this doesn't mean you're exercising unjustifiable favoritism.

Promote Spending Time Together

By sharing positive experiences, people become more bonded. Therefore, it's crucial to provide opportunities for siblings to enjoy themselves together.

Take note of the activities they like to do and the times when they play well together, whether they like to color together or go play in the park. After that, deliberately plan more of these activities to promote bonding.

When there are significant age gaps or when your children have wildly dissimilar interests, this can be a little challenging. However, there are always ways to encourage good time spent together; you may just need to be a little inventive.

Children feel happier when they are laughing and enjoying themselves. Additionally, they will feel better about one another when they share these positive emotions with their siblings.

Decide on regular family-friendly activities to plan. And make sure you time it just right. When they are hungry, cranky, or overtired, expecting them to play nicely may not go as planned..

promoting cooperation over rivalry

Pitting the kids against one another is a bad idea, despite the fact that you might feel like the family can be more productive when you say things like, "Let's see who can clean their room the fastest.".

Place more emphasis on collaboration than on rivalry. Discuss how you are all on the same team and how you can support one another. Each member of the family can learn to cooperate when you work as a unit.

Instead of saying, "Let's not be the last person out the door," you might say, "Let's see how we can all get out the door on time this morning."

Give them tasks they can complete together, such as designing a card for Grandma or finishing a scavenger hunt. Encourage them to realize that they perform better as a team and without having to compete for your attention.

Instead of praising their performance, commend their cooperation and effort. Don't mention who took the best photo or got the most points. Use phrases like "I really like the way you two are working together" or "I appreciate that you're helping your brother with this project" as an alternative. You're so sweet, that.

Healthy Conflict Resolution Model

Sibling arguments are a great way for kids to practice conflict resolution, negotiation, and other skills.

When it is healthy to do so, let them practice compromising, sharing, and listening. It's sometimes preferable to take a back seat and let them settle things amicably rather than mediating every dispute.

But if one child is being mistreated or picked on, it's crucial to intervene. Sibling bullying is a significant issue. According to studies, bullying between siblings has a negative psychological impact and may even increase a teen's propensity for self-harm. 10

Don't simply shout, "Stop fighting!" from the adjacent room. They make learning opportunities out of their disagreements.

When you must intervene, set a good example for effective conflict resolution. Together, they find constructive solutions to problems.

"You both want to play with the same toy." How can you help? Then, you might decide that each person gets 10 minutes to play with it. Alternately, you might decide that they will use the toy together.

Make a mission statement for your family

A straightforward family mission statement can assist in reminding everyone of the essentials in life. It can serve as a reminder to the children of their shared objective..

Your mission statement might simply read, "Our family values showing kindness to others. And even in difficult times, we put in a lot of effort; alternatively, "The Smith family never gives up."

Your mission statement should be written down and posted on the wall. Repeat it frequently and give specific instances of how you're collaborating to complete your mission..

Request examples from the children's everyday experiences as well. When you have a common goal, your entire family may feel more unified.

Create Rituals

According to a study that appeared in the Journal of Family Psychology, family rituals or traditions are linked to better marital satisfaction, a stronger sense of identity during adolescence, and stronger family ties.

Family customs are which isolate your family from the remainder of the world. Whether you appreciate "Taco Tuesdays" together or you observe Valentine's Day with chocolate hotcakes, laying out customs can assist everybody with feeling nearer.

Family customs are likewise an extraordinary method for making enduring recollections. The children will constantly recollect how they had film night each Friday or how the family generally went to the ocean side on the main day of summer.

Normal outcomes assist jokes with figuring out how to use sound judgment. For example, assuming that a youngster is told to take care of their walkway chalk however leaves it outside during a rainstorm, a characteristic result would be that it gets generally wet (or it could get taken). In the event that a youngster is reminded to carry a sweater to school, however doesn't, they may be crisp in their cool homerooms.

As a parent, it's enticing to simply take care of your youngster's chalk for them or rush in with the sweater. Yet, assuming you do as such, your kid will not become familiar with the strong examples that normal outcomes can instruct. While it may very well be difficult to allow your youngster to go with an unfortunate decision and experience the aftereffects of their activities, permitting them to confront the regular results gives them the required information and inspiration to improve sometime later.

The extraordinary thing about ingraining normal results is you don't need to do a lot to allow them to do something amazing. All things being equal, you fundamentally need to move and allow your kid to encounter the implications of their slips up — for however long it's protected to do as such. Get familiar with how to utilize normal results to oversee and direct your kid's way of behaving..

What Are Natural Consequences?

Basically, regular outcomes essentially occur because of an individual's activities, with practically no intercession by an external party. As a matter of fact, the way to utilize normal outcomes with kids is for the parent to move to one side and permit their kid to encounter the impact of what they've done or not done.

By not mediating when a kid slips up, the parent allows the youngster to advance by genuinely encountering their rewards for so much hard work. This might imply that they end up crisp, overtired, without their schoolwork, late, or quite a few other undesirable things. They might feel disheartened or disappointed. They might bomb a test or lose a thing that they forgot at school. While it's difficult to allow your youngster to feel these things, the point is for them to gain from these encounters.

Consistent versus Regular Consequences

"Normal outcomes are things that happen consequently because of a kid's activity or inaction with practically no intentional conduct on the grown-up's part," "In the event that the regular result is undesirable or disagreeable, the youngster has the potential chance to gain from the experience and do things any other way the next opportunity to keep away from the unsavory experience."

Instances of Natural Consequences

Chances to utilize regular outcomes flourish. "For instance, a preschooler who bounces in a puddle will feel cold and awkward until the end of the trip home. A tween who is responsible for their own clothing will not have the option to take part in a game [if their uniform isn't clean]. A youngster who goes out with friends as opposed to studying for a test will normally wind up with a lower grade,".

That's what different conceivable outcomes include. Assuming your youngster stays up past the point of no return, they will be drained the following day. A kid who is responsible for preparing their lunch will be eager in the event that they just bring an apple or granola bar to school. "A youngster who leaves a toy outside will not have the option to play with it any longer in the event that it is taken or broken,". Furthermore, in the event that a youngster lies, they will lose trust or honor. For example, in the event that your kid says they emptied the dishwasher yet didn't, they probably won't procure their recompense.

The Advantages of Natural Consequences

There are enormous advantages to utilizing normal outcomes with your youngsters. This methodology, first and foremost, shows your youngster obligation, freedom, and inspiration.

It encourages intrinsic motivation

When guardians regularly rush in to get things done for their children as well as "salvage" them from their activities (or inaction), they are denied the ability to create inspiration to deal with their own necessities. "Regular results can assist kids with creating characteristic inspiration for acting in versatile ways," On the off chance that they realize you will not fix it assuming they neglect to do what is generally anticipated, they will turn out to be significantly more liable to do what should be done by themselves.

At the point when a kid completes their book report, since you bothered them to make it happen, that is outer inspiration. In the event that they do it all alone in light of the fact that they need to get a passing mark or for the fulfillment of finishing their work, that is characteristic inspiration. Normal outcomes help to assemble this kind of interior resolution that will work well for youngsters later on.

On the off chance that they don't invest the effort, the regular outcome is genuinely regretting turning in disappointing work and getting a lower grade, results that might spur them to improve sometime later. If you "fix it" for them by doing the report with (or for) them, they're denied this experience and may not foster the characteristic inspiration to go about their own responsibilities.

It creates autonomy

Regular results assist me with turning out to be more free and confident. "They assist kids with taking on obligations and finding out how they have some control over results through their own decisions," she said. "Subsequent to encountering an undesirable normal outcome, the youngster can utilize the learned data the next time what is happening happens. "Conduct might change once the youngster comprehends and encounters the undesirable result."

Here and there, it tends to be precarious to recognize how your youngster ought to or shouldn't turn out to be more autonomous. "As guardians contemplate independence support, ask yourself, 'Are they fit to do it without anyone's help?' If in this way, let them make it happen," says Dr. Pressman. What's more, let them feel the consequences on the off chance that they don't make it happen (or do it the correct way).

It demonstrates cause and effect

When you utilize normal results, the objective isn't just the distress the kid might experience, but instead that they foster a comprehension of circumstances and logical results, can make forecasts, and can comprehend their own capacity to affect their current circumstance, says Dr. Fulton. On the off chance that you spare children from encountering normal results, as guardians might feel a sense of urgency to do on occasion, they are denied the opportunity to make the association between their activities and what occurs because of their activities.

In the event that a kid doesn't set their caution, they will be late. On the off chance that they don't get back to their companion, they might wind up with practically no friendly exercises at the end of the week. Thus, they'll see that they have the power to affect what occurs in their lives—adversely and emphatically. Moreover, rather than the kid following through with something (say putting on a coat) in light of the fact that their parent tells them to, they figure out how to do it due to the ideal outcome (not being crisp when it's chilly outside).

Step by step, Step-by-step instructions to use Positive and Negative Consequences

When children are permitted to have normal ramifications for their activities, they might probably have a few unfavorable encounters. In any case, in addition to that, they have the opportunity to develop and gain from these circumstances. Therefore, you can assist them with chipping away at their adaptive abilities, critical thinking abilities, and flexibility. By providing assistance, you can direct them on the most effective way to solve the problem—and how to improve it later. elected to hit up their closest companion's birthday celebration or to bring a birthday present, those slips up may influence the kinship. By providing assistance, you can direct them on the most effective way to solve the problem—and how to improve it later. They should learn to adapt to a companion being angry with them or to the failure of missing a get-together.

On the off chance that they miss the cutoff time for pursuing a school club, they might pass up that open door. Living with the results of their activities assists in inspiring them to be more capable and proactive next time. This allows them the opportunity to adapt to a sensible disillusionment as well as to make a move to correct the circumstance. This sort of involvement might develop flexibility that they can draw from when other sad things occur not too far off.

When to Use Natural Consequences

Open doors for normal results come up frequently; simply make certain to possibly utilize them when it's safe and formatively suitable. Frequently, they work best with more established youngsters, but they can likewise be compelling with more youthful children insofar as doing so is protected and they are mature enough to figure out the effect. "In the event that you end up enticed to meditate on something your kid is liable for or to prevent them from following through with something, it may be a great chance to consider what the normal outcome would be in the event that you didn't act. " In the event that the outcome is horrendous, but not destructive or hazardous, it is possible for the kid to encounter and gain from a characteristic result,"

Instructions to Choose Appropriate Consequences for Kids

When to Avoid Natural Consequences

While regular results can give strong learning opportunities, there are times when they ought not be utilized. Specifically, they aren't suitable when security is an issue or for infants or extremely small kids who aren't fully grown to comprehend or go with these choices for themselves.

If it doesn't appear to be appropriate or safe, try another discipline system; occasionally, removing honors or putting a child on break is more powerful.

Regular results don't operate admirably on more youthful kids. Generally, young children and preschoolers miss the mark in their capacity to comprehend that the outcome is an immediate consequence of their behavior. For instance, in the event that you let a 4-year-old pick their own sleep time, they probably won't realize they're worn out on the grounds that they remained up past the point of no return. Except if they comprehend circumstances and logical results, they aren't probably going to pick a previous sleep time in the future all alone. Ensure your youngster can perceive the association and afterwards apply that example to their future way of behaving. Most tweens and young people ought to have the option to perceive how their conduct prompted an outcome.

Ensure It's Safe,

Normal results ought to be utilized when it is safe to do as such. Obviously, infants and small kids need their folks to deal with their own requirements and can't be expected to take on any obligations before they're formatively prepared, for example, trying not to have a mishap before they are completely latrine prepared.

Try not to permit your youngster to use a kitchen blade solo to "show them a thing or two." They could be truly harmed. All things considered, when there's a potential wellbeing issue or something that could cause angreater than they ought to be liable for, mediate before your youngster commits an error. Make sense of why this conduct is inadmissible and, when fundamental, totally finish a consistent result.

For instance, in the event that a kid is liable for strolling or taking care of their canine but doesn't finish, you'll have to step in to ensure the canine

　　　　　10 Minutes To Become A Better Parent

gets the attention they need. Thus, rather than a characteristic outcome (that the canine goes hungry or goes to the restroom in the house), pick one more strategy to show your youngster their preferred repercussions. For instance, they could need to skip playing at the recreation area or lose screen time.

For instance, on the off chance that a kid is making toast yet neglects to haul it out of the toaster oven or leaves it in excessively long, they might wind up eating cool toast that the spread won't dissolve into or consume toast. On the off chance that they make their cereal yet don't destroy it right, it is saturated. On the off chance that they don't get up on occasion in the first part of the day, they may not be in a hurry to wash up and make breakfast. These are times when regular outcomes are suitable.

Avoiding any "no real surprises there" while utilizing regular consequences is significant." "Normal outcomes will be best when the grown-up permits them to occur without adding affront." or judgment. " Guardians are frequently enticed to express something with the impact of, 'See?' or 'Look what you did.' Instead, being casual yet empathic in response is generally useful,".

Parenting Skills to be Followed Globally

1. Get to the Root of the Behavior

Positive nurturing specialists overall can settle on this: there is continuously something spurring a kid's negative or troublesome way of behaving. So fit over the blue plate? It was anything but an irregular showcase of misguided thinking - it was persuaded by something characteristically in your kid. Whether that was an absence of abilities in dealing with his enormous sentiments, a craving to stand out, or a strategic maneuver to declare his unrestrained choice - there's dependably a justification behind the way of behaving. (Regardless of whether he understands it - and most times he doesn't!)

What to recollect is the actual conduct is basically the side effect. Our test as guardians is sorting out what's truly under that baffling way of behaving. It would make things MUCH more straightforward if your kid would essentially say, "Mom, I would truly like somebody one- on-one consideration with you when I have you all to myself. Is there a period we can do that tonight?" But we as a whole realize this is a silly assumption. So all things being equal, youngsters irritate us as a method for acquiring our consideration, yet negative. Since truly, on the off chance that a kid doesn't accept our consideration in certain ways, (when they don't need to ask for or request it) they will track down ways of standing out enough to be noticed they can, even if it's negative.

Imagine yourself as an investigator. When a youngster starts to carry on, ask yourself "What is this kid attempting to achieve through his activities?" If he had the verbal abilities and profound mindfulness, "What might he be attempting to tell me with this way of behaving?"

When you recognize the underlying driver of the issue, you can turn into a more PROACTIVE parent and stop the explosions from occurring in any case.

For instance, imagine you need to accept a significant call, however while you're on the telephone, your kids choose it's an extraordinary opportunity to begin a wrestling match. While actually attempting to sound participated in the telephone discussion, you give your children the "in the event that you don't stop this right presently I will lose it when I'm finished" look - however without any result. You go on with the non-verbal shushing as you run starting with one room then onto the next looking for calm, however the wrestling match appears to follow you. It's depleting. What's more, toward the finish of the call, you feel like you just ran 5 miles.

The objective behind that wrestling match - that coincidentally started the moment you got on the telephone - was probably planned to definitely stand out and provoke you. They realized you were caught on the telephone and unfit to mediate, so it turned into the ideal chance to misbehave, definitely standing out in bad ways. Utilize this as an opportunity for growth and presently PROACTIVELY PREPARE for the following time you really want to accept a call.

20 minutes before your call, say to your youngsters, "Hello folks, mom needs to get on the telephone shortly. That's what I do, I couldn't want anything more than to play a game with all of you!" During those 20 minutes paving the way to the call, actually focus on your kids. You can surrender them updates prompting the refer to like as "Goodness! I love messing around with you. Whenever mama is done with her call, I'd very much want to play once more!"

At the point when it comes time for the call, give your youngsters a decision - "Mom needs to get on her call now. Might you want to watch a show or play discreetly with your legos while I'm on the telephone?" Likewise, give them a way to "let you know something" on the off chance that something they view as dire comes up while you're on the call. Leave a stack of paper close by so they can compose or attract anything they desire to tell you when your call is done.

Odds are in the event that you fill their consideration pails early and spread out clear assumptions, your kids will be better acted next time you accept a call.

2. Be Consistent

While guardians mentally comprehend the significance of consistency, in all actuality, life occurs - school is dropped, plans change, augmentations are made to the schedule last-minute. While we can't necessarily in every case control life occurring, it's ideal to keep up with reliable schedules, timetables, and assumptions in your home most of the time.

How is your morning schedule? Assuming your kids are supposed to make their beds, clean their teeth and get dressed prior to having breakfast, then keep up with this schedule consistently.

Star TIP: Maintain the SAME timetable on ends of the week and occasions. Like that, you will not need to encounter the break faith that comes on Monday morning!

Do you keep up with firm innovation "approaches?" What occurs in the event that your children don't regard your family rules for innovation? To be the positive parent you endeavor to be, it's fundamental that innovation rules are obviously conveyed and that children know the result assuming those rules are broken. Assuming children reject or "neglect" to switch off the computer game when time is up, completely finish every single time with the recently talked about result. At the point when guardians are steady with the standards and results, kids are significantly less liable to stretch the boundaries.

3.Say No to Rewards

Guardians who are new to positive nurturing procedures are much of the time amazed when I deter them from utilizing rewards. All things considered, rewards sound positive, however truly they cause more damage than great and can prompt a significant portion of qualification not too far off. Nurturing is a long distance race, not a run. While settling on discipline choices for your children, remembering your drawn out objectives is significant. Rewards are ineffectual on the grounds that they just proposition momentary addition. Contemplate it..maybe today you compensated your kid with a treat for acting great in the supermarket, yet what will she anticipate sometime later? Something like one treat, isn't that so? Perhaps two? Will a comparative prize be normal during the following specialist's office visit or excursion to the shopping center?

Or on the other hand maybe you paid off your finicky eater to eat their vegetables by offering frozen yogurt for dessert? Now that he realizes vegetables can be sold at the cost of frozen yogurt, it just checks out he would hold out on eating his greens until he's offered frozen yogurt or another similarly engaging sweet award.

Involving compensations as a negotiating concession for the ideal way of behaving is a dangerous slant to a demeanor of qualification.

4. Center Around What You Can Control - YOURSELF

Gracious my companions, this one is extreme, particularly seemingly out of the blue. However, assuming you recall that there's dependably a REASON for the way of behaving AND your kids have freedom of thought, then you can start to suitably answer.

All things considered, there is a degree of close to home opportunity that is found when guardians understand "I can't necessarily control my children, however I have some control over my reactions."

Certainly, a few guardians could possibly unnerve their children into acting appropriately or undermine discipline to accomplish a foolhardy objective, however by the day's end - every youngster will develop into a grown-up who has full command over their important choices.

So rather than overwhelming kids, or paying off, or disgracing them into using sound judgment, I urge guardians to reexamine their view of the kid. Rather than considering him a getting out of hand kid, view him as a little individual who essentially hasn't been furnished with the right devices to act fittingly in a given circumstance. By doing this, guardians will be more ready to deal with the mischievous activities.

One way we have some control over our reactions is to conclude what we're willing to do AHEAD OF TIME. This turns out perfect for getting children to take on liabilities they're entirely adequate of or we bother them about, yet they regularly don't do - exhausting knapsacks or lunchboxes, placing clothing in the hamper, tidying up toys, and so on.

We should utilize lunchboxes for instance.

Begin by concluding what you're willing to do, and what age-suitable obligation should be on your children's shoulders. In a quiet second, uncover ahead of time, "I'm glad to make you a lunch each day for school, as long as your lunchbox has been purged out, and it's on the rack in the storage space or on the counter. On the off chance that the lunchboxes are perfect and in their place, I'm glad to make your lunch. In the event that it's not cleared out or not in its place, it'll really depend on you to make your own lunch." Then inquire, "Is there anything you might want to do to assist yourself with making sure to empty your lunchbox and put it in the storeroom?" (He should make a sign in pictures or words to remind himself since you won't remind.)

Furthermore, obviously - ensure everybody has an unmistakable way of getting it: "To make sure we're in total agreement, might you at any point echo once again to me your obligation regarding lunch boxes and what I've concluded I will do about making snacks?" Right now, you've prepared and engaged your kid, you've uncovered what could occur, and you've let your kid know what you will do. The subsequent stage is to see everything through to completion. This part will be hard - however kindly don't remind them or bother them - in any case, this turns into YOUR concern once more. On the off chance that the lunchbox is spotless and on the rack - extraordinary, you'll make the lunch. If not, it will create a superb learning open door sometime later. At the point when you can proactively PREPARE your reactions to possible dilemmas and obviously COMMUNICATE your assumptions in advance, you'll end up responding to circumstances without giving it much thought.

Good parenting can mean different things to different people. Parenting is a skill that can be learned and improved over time, despite the fact that there are no set standards or laws. Being a good parent doesn't require you to always get it right or to be perfect. More importantly, you should take on these significant responsibilities as practically and kindly as you can.

Your parenting style will have a big influence on how your child develops. In order to be a good parent, you must make decisions that are in your child's best interests. It also entails bringing up your child with tolerance, affection, wisdom, direction, and nurturing. Different people may have different parenting styles. What works for one kid or family might not be the best option for another. The good news is that there are ways for anyone, regardless of who they are, to learn how to be a good parent. You might find the following advice useful.

Set a good example

One of the most frequent mistakes parents make is telling their kids what to do without also setting an example for those behaviors. Little children look up to their parents and other influential adults. Children often mimic actions they see adults doing. Because your child closely observes everything you do, be sure to "walk the talk." Children have a natural tendency to imitate others, especially their parents.

It's crucial that you demonstrate these traits yourself if you want to raise your child to be a respectful, kind, and loving person. Make sure you don't spend a lot of time on your screen or stay up all night binge-watching your favorite shows if you want your child to have limited screen time. Make sure to set an example for healthy eating in your own life if you want your child to eat well.

Use your actions to express your love and affection

'Spoiling' your child is not the same as loving them. You can discipline your child and teach them appropriate behaviors while still loving them.

A child's basic needs include attention from their parents, feelings of love and care, and an understanding and sense of being heard. Make sure your child knows how much you love him or her by telling them. Along with verbal affirmations, small actions like handshakes and hugs can have a big impact. You should always be available to them in times of need, pay attention to their requirements, spend time with them, and listen to their experiences and sentiments. Keep in mind that they desire your love and presence more than anything else.

Be compassionate while remaining firm

It can be challenging to discipline kids in the right way. Parents occasionally struggle to discipline their children because they are either "too soft" or "too harsh." Unbelievably, a parent can be both firm and kind in their treatment of their children. Trying to discipline your child and instill good behavior in them can be challenging, but discipline doesn't always have to mean using harsh punishment..

Positive discipline can help in this situation. There are several alternatives to using physical punishment to discipline a child. If your child displays challenging behavior, for instance, putting them in time-out is an example of a nonviolent form of discipline.

Control your own tension and rage

As parents, we can all agree that it can be challenging to control our own stress and rage. Even though it's common for us to become upset and frustrated during stressful situations, it's crucial that we learn effective stress and anger management techniques. These kinds of negative emotions can have a negative impact on our interactions with our children when we let them consume us. When in a challenging situation, try to maintain your composure. If necessary, you can even leave and take a break. When you're under a lot of stress, the last thing you want is for your child to see you snap.

Remember to take care of your own physical and mental health.

You can't pour from an empty cup, as the saying goes. This also holds true for parenting. As parents, we occasionally juggle too many duties and wear too many hats, which can leave us with almost no time for ourselves. No matter how much you want to provide for the needs of your children and family, it's important to remember to look after your own needs and wellbeing. The way you relate to your kids can be greatly affected by how well you take care of yourself, both physically and mentally. Make loving yourself a top priority.

Being a good parent is challenging. Bringing up children is not an easy task. You can improve your parenting abilities and navigate parenthood more easily with the aid of these suggestions.

Parenting has its share of difficulties and difficulties. The pandemic and the political climate have made day-to-day coping a major concern for everyone, as if times weren't already difficult enough.

Parenting techniques for babies and toddlers may thus be challenging to put into practice. This might also apply to older children. However, you can use these suggestions for good parenting techniques to maintain a PRIDE-like home environment. Praise, Reflection, Imitation, Description, and Enjoyment are the letters in the word pride.

Positive comments that express support are considered praise. Any comments made to children at any age become their internal dialogue. This voice has the power to strengthen or undermine. Self-confidence is increased by encouragement.

The development of a child's social and problem-solving skills is supported by positive communication. Additionally, it strengthens connections with caregivers and peers. A child is more likely to believe in themselves and their future when their parents are upbeat and supportive of them.

Allowing toddlers and young children to assist with feeding and getting dressed can help them develop their independence.

Let them know that while each attempt may not be perfect, it is still worthwhile. Encourage them to set attainable goals as they get older. They will develop a sense of self-worth and become less dependent on praise or rewards.

Teenagers should have their opinions respected and their feelings and thought processes taken into account. Feeling "heard" and understood by you is crucial.

Praise should be given for effort as well as work, not just results. Respect the need for autonomy and a little privacy as well.

Consideration: Be receptive

Positive psychology is a parenting style that emphasizes nurturing good behavior rather than focusing on bad behavior. Being receptive to your children is the first step. When they feel appreciated and supported, kids behave in healthy ways. Children who have emotionally open parents who act as their coaches gain more advantages than those who don't.

Talk to babies when possible. Your voice will be comforting to them. To encourage language learning, repeat sounds your baby makes and add words. As your children get older, assist them by guiding them through a problem-solving process when they become upset.

Make it a point to visit with them as they get older. Discuss their acquaintances, successes, and any difficulties they may be experiencing. Thank them for identifying triggers.

Respond to older teens' worries while keeping an eye out for any behavior changes. Inquiring about their level of sadness, depression, or suicidal thoughts is acceptable. If so, help your teen to seek help. This aids in preventing issues before they worsen.

Impersonation: Lead by example

A parent mimicking a child can be endearing and convey the message that you value and value them, and that you aspire to be like them. Children are likely to mimic adults when they imitate children. This is a good way to encourage social interactions in younger children.

There are many advantageous effects when a parent develops in a manner that is instructive, supportive, and loving. These results consist of:

- higher compliance
- additional school readiness
- more favorable social and cognitive growth
- willingness to experiment
- Less toxicity
- reduced antisocial behavior

Encourage pretend play with your young child. Play along and switch from inappropriate to appropriate behavior.

When your child faces new challenges, encourage them. Be present when issues arise and promote problem-solving.

When discussing touchy subjects with teenagers, such as drinking, smoking, sex, and drugs, be straightforward. Be a role model at the same time and avoid saying things and acting differently.

Description: Establish boundaries... but definitely

You should find w when practicing positive parenting. To enforce the value of rules, be explicit about your subsequent actions after crossing boundaries. Show how adhering to the rules produces positive results.

Children can tell you have their attention when you use descriptions. They will know you are interested, which will help them feel better about themselves. Setting limits and consequences demonstrates accountability and responsibility. When boundaries and consequences are made clear in advance, a child will appreciate the importance of adhering to the rules. Consequences should not shock them.

No matter what, boundaries and rules should be communicated in a constructive manner.

Pay attention to your children and praise them when they follow directions. Pay attention to good behavior and try to avoid drawing attention to negative actions like temper tantrums. Teach your child alternative ways to express their angst. Reward kids for having positive attitudes. It is best to focus praise on the child's accomplishments rather than on what they didn't do. What a great job you did figuring this out, for instance.

When there is a conflict, be clear about expectations and goals for older children. Listen to their suggestions on how they think a goal should be accomplished while demonstrating respect and keeping your position of authority.

Be interactive for enjoyment

When you are with your child, enjoyment means exuding warmth and positivity through your actions and words.

Among the ways to convey enjoyment through body language are:

- maintaining gaze
- your child in your arms

- Smiling

- Hugs and kisses

Positive parenting outcomes can result from parents' interventions that convey enjoyment. Enjoyment enhances school adjustment and attachment security. It increases competency and causes many problematic behaviors to change.

Positive parenting is exciting, which reduces stress and conflict in families.It improves family communication and organization. It reduces problematic behaviors and increases optimistic development. It reduces problematic behaviors while fostering more positive growth. to understand and regulate their own emotions. A child's creativity, self-esteem, relationship goals, future goals, and overall sense of wellbeing are all increased by many aspects of positive parenting.

A parent who is encouraging, nurturing, and loving equips their child with the knowledge and abilities necessary to take on challenges head-on and develop into a truly well-rounded individual. Your concern about what technology is doing to children is one that is shared by the majority of parents. Spending a lot of time on phones: Do they use social media too much? Do they have interpersonal communication skills? In fact, research demonstrates how reliant children are on technology and the impact this has on them. For instance, the use of technology by this generation is causing an increase in bullying, a decline in empathy, and a loss of creativity. In fact, according to universities and businesses, children who have grown up in this technologically advanced world lack emotional maturity compared to children a decade ago.

What then, should a parent do? As a form of discipline, parents frequently create cell phone contracts, place time restrictions on screen use, set timers, and take away technology. What if, instead, the problem with technology, social media, and the Internet in our children's lives is more to do with how much we parents allow our own technology to obstruct our ability to parent? What if checking social media and email prevents our children from having important interactions with us?

They want to talk to us or ask us a challenging question, but we are preoccupied with checking our phones, responding to work emails, or browsing social media. So when they see the gadget, in our hands, they either give up or turn to the Internet to look up the solution. We lose out on important parenting opportunities when this occurs.

You aren't emotionally connected

Additionally, study participants reported that their emotional reactions to what they read on their mobile devices frequently caused them to react negatively toward their family members, particularly when the email or message they were reading contained unfavorable information or was stressful. Parents reported that their kids tended to act more attention-seeking when they were immersed in technology, which led to them losing their cool with them.

In a different section of the study, the researchers watched parents consuming food with their kids in fast-food establishments. They found that when using mobile devices around children, there are fewer verbal and nonverbal reactions.

Growing Children

It Turns Into a Way to Get Away

Others who took part in the study defended their use of technology by saying that it provided them with a connection to the outside world and was an important reminder that there is life outside of being a parent. Numerous parents also mentioned using technology to escape the monotony and boredom that can accompany parenting. In total, parents are thought to spend up to three hours per day using mobile devices like smartphones, wearables, and tablets.

The researchers noted that parents are overburdened and exhausted from being pulled in so many different directions, even though they acknowledge that parents do not have to be available to their children 100% of the time and that children develop independence with some alone time. Additionally, technology has changed how parents interact with their children.

Technology demands more of a parent's attention and an emotional commitment than conventional books, newspapers, or magazines do.As a result, there is less of you available to invest in your children as a result of this significant emotional investment.

Controlling Your Use of Technology

Researchers provide some advice on how to manage your technology use. Setting family boundaries, keeping track of your mobile usage, and figuring out your main device stressors are some of these.

Make the Right Inquiries

You need to be honest with yourself if you truly want to control how you use technology. How frequently do you, for instance, take out your phone during dinner to check your email or reply to a text? How much time do you spend uploading pictures and selfies to social media instead of being present in the moment? Alternatively, how much time do you spend documenting your children's lives on social media rather than genuinely spending time with them? You will be able to see where changes need to be made once you have critically examined your own behavior.

Establish Limits

Plan out how you're going to use technology. You could, for instance, designate specific areas of your home or times of day when you completely unplug. The obvious options include not using a device at the breakfast or dinner table, or when your children are in their rooms at night. You could also designate certain areas of your home, like the family room or the reading room, as technology-free zones.

Monitor your mobile activity

Utilizing an app like Moment or Quality Time to monitor your mobile usage is a good idea. With the aid of this information, you can determine when and where you are spending excessive amounts of time. As a result, you can look for ways to cut back on your technology use if you find that 90 percent of your time is spent on social media or reading work emails. To resist the temptation to use technology when family members arrive home from school, you arrive home from work, or it's time for bed, you could also set up a filter or block on your device.

Determine Stressors

One of the main issues parents bring up is that occasionally using a mobile device can make them irritable or snap at their kids. Think back to a time in your life when this occurred. Plan times to do these things when you know your kids are occupied with sports or another activity, if you get stressed out reading work emails or need complete silence to focus on a project for work. Instead of taking time away from your children or running the risk of snapping at them when they interrupt you with a question, you will have the room and time you require to finish your tasks in this manner.

Assist Kids With finding the Benefit of Quiet

Too often, innovation is continuously running. The iPad is playing recordings or the PC has a YouTube video on it. Yet, research has shown that tranquil time without the obstruction of innovation is urgent to mind development.6 Think about your own circumstance. How often have you been collapsing clothing or scrubbing down and think of a good thought for a task at work? It is during these peaceful times that our minds are permitted to be generally innovative. Show your children the significance of calm by displaying it yourself. Switch off your gadget and walk the canine. Oppose turning on the TV while you are collapsing clothing. In the event that your children see you do these things, they are bound to display your way of behaving.

Use "Caught" Time to Talk

Riding in the vehicle, finding a seat during supper, gathering at an eatery - those times all address "caught" time with your children. Thus, you need to exploit that time and set the gadgets aside. For example, kids are more pleasing to chat with you when you are riding in the vehicle. They don't need to visually engage with you, particularly on the off chance that you are discussing a troublesome or humiliating point. They can glance through the window assuming they need. In this way, consider making short vehicle rides to rehearses, to chapel, or to the grandparents' home innovation free. Along these lines, you can exploit that opportunity to talk. You wouldn't believe what you could find while riding in the vehicle.

Make a Technology Basket

Put a bin by the entryway where your family comes in and out and place your gadgets in that container when you return home. Request that your children do likewise. The innovation emerges from the container when schoolwork is finished, supper is done, and errands are finished - anything that rules you need to lay out. Along these lines, you have restricted interruptions during vital correspondence time for both you and the children.

Give Other Options

Too often, guardians depend on innovation to make up for the shortcoming during the day for themselves as well as for their children too. One thought for decreasing innovation use for the whole family is to give different choices in the home. For example, put a couple of prepackaged games or a deck of cards on the table. Set a ball or frisbee by the entryway. Spread out Mad Libs or word search books on the foot stool. On the off chance that these things are in full view, children (and guardians) are bound to make the most of them as opposed to going to innovation for amusement.

Make Media Viewing a Family Event

Watch things along with your children and afterward discuss them a while later. For example, on the off chance that your children like watching a specific film or YouTuber, watch with them. Then have a discussion subsequently. Consider how these things meet with your family values. In addition to the fact that you doing are something with your children, yet you likewise are showing them how to involve innovation in a manner that expects them to contemplate what they are observing as opposed to just consuming it.

Put Your Technology Down

Indeed, that's all there was to it. Assuming your children see you restricting your innovation use or leaving for your screen to accomplish something different, they will probably imitate these activities in their own lives. Kids advance as a visual cue more than anything more. Furthermore, assuming you effectively put down certain boundaries on your own innovation use (counting not utilizing your telephone while driving) then they are probably going to do likewise.

Be Intentional

All in all, conclude what you believe your family should resemble. Then, at that point, in light of this image, put forth objectives and make an arrangement. There is no ideal response or a particular line to attract with regards to innovation and nurturing. Thus, you need to exercise common decency for yourself as well as your loved ones.

Innovation has changed the manner in which parents collaborate with their youngsters. From having children and teenagers fastened to their gadgets and being in consistent contact with guardians, to parting consideration between their children and their cell phones, nurturing doesn't look like it did 10 years prior. A portion of these advancements are beneficial things, such as having the option to message your children when they are out.

However, some of these progressions are affecting the manner in which guardians speak with their children in a negative way. All things considered, it is reasonable. With just the right amount of exertion and a promise to be completely present, parents can undoubtedly make innovation work for them instead of against them.

Model Healthy Electronic Use

Guardians should be good examples of screen use for their kids. Before you marathon watch your #1 Netflix series, recollect that you are setting a model for your children with your own time spent before a screen.

Keeping the TV on for foundation commotion constantly or looking at your telephone any time you have an extra moment may not be demonstrating the screen-related conduct you desire to find in your children.

Teach Yourself on Electronics

The present children are educated. A larger portion of them find out about gadgets than grown-ups do. Guardians need to keep awake to-date on the most recent applications, games, and virtual entertainment stages, and patterns.

For instance, you can't show your kid the dangers of web-based entertainment except if you figure out the perils yourself. In like manner, you wouldn't have the option to keep them from consuming specific kinds of media, (for example, brutal computer games) in the event that you fail to really see how these types of media are rated.

Make "Innovation Free Zones"

Lay out zones in your home where hardware is not permitted — whether it's mobile phones, handheld computer games, or PCs. One example is your home's lounge area or kitchen, which you could keep for having feasts and family discussions.

Put Away Times to Unplug

Put away time for your entire family to turn off their mechanical devices. Dinnertime or an hour prior to sleep time are two models. When all of you consent to save your gadgets, it offers your family the chance to spend insightful, quality time together.

Utilize Parental Controls

There are devices you can use to shield your children from getting to express happiness on the Internet and on TV.Most switches, internet browsers, and TVs have parental controls that you can get up in a position channel or block undesirable substances.

Assuming your children have cell phones, there are likewise implicit settings or applications you can download that permit you to create content channels. Many also permit you to obstruct explicit sites, web searches, or even watchwords.

Make sense of why you're Limiting screen time

Assuming your children comprehend that you're restricting your family's screen time on the grounds that a lot of time spent on screens has drawbacks, they're substantially more likely to observe the guidelines you set. On the off chance that your children simply believe you're not kidding," "they may be bound to oppose or defy the guidelines you are attempting to uphold.

In light of what's proper for your kid's age, make sense of why brutal video games, TV shows, and motion pictures can be harmful. If your children utilize the Internet, ensure you have a discussion with them about the risks of online hunters.

Ensure that each individual from your family is remembered for the conversation about screen time and are essential for making a list of limits that everybody can follow.

Request Your Child's Passwords

You should consider asking your children for the passwords to their virtual entertainment accounts. Kids don't necessarily have the development necessary to deal with online collaborations and can be defenseless against cyberbullying.

You'll have to examine the choice as a family, but it will ultimately depend on you as the parent to sort out the most ideal way to assist with safeguarding your kid while as yet permitting them to have some protection and independence.

Empower Other Activities

With an abundance of applications, games, gadgets, and content, it's simple for youngsters to become dependent on hardware for diversion.

Urge your kid to search out and engage in exercises that needn't bother with a screen. Playing outside, perusing a book, or, in any event, recovering an old tabletop game are only a couple of thoughts.

It can likewise assist with laying out (and implementing) a timetable that everybody in your home follows. Making it clear to your children when they are permitted on screens and when they are not will assist with explaining your assumptions and can forestall contention.

1. Put down stopping points

Having limits in our relationship with our kids is critical to finding success in sure nurturing. Having, and authorizing, limits permits us to stay patient and quiet since we feel regarded and that our necessities in the relationship are being met.

An effective method for knowing when you really want to lay out another limit is the point at which you are feeling exasperated, fretful or furious by a repetitive way of behaving or circumstance.

Do you fear supper time in light of the fact that your kid demands sitting on your lap and you mightn't? Provided that this is true, lay out a standard that everybody sits in their own seat for feasts. You can cuddle after supper.

Do you feel angry on the grounds that your kid implores you to play dolls first thing each day when your eyes aren't as yet even open?

Lay out a standard that you get to sit and drink espresso for 10 minutes before you're free to play. Will your kid gripe? Likely. However, they will likewise start to discover that you have needs as well.

You will be a superior parent in the event that your own requirements are being met and your kid will see a superb illustration of how to advocate for their own necessities in a relationship.

2. Assemble association with gain participation

Do you had a substitute educator as a youngster? Did anybody pay attention to them? Most likely not. Youngsters need to feel an association with a grown-up to pay attention to them. This is something worth being thankful for — you don't need your kid paying attention to any irregular more odd who instructs them to follow through with something.

Yet, it likewise implies your kid is bound to pay attention to you when they feel associated with you. This is the issue with discipline. It puts you in conflict with your kid, decreasing your association and making it doubtful your kid will do what you inquire.

In the event that your youngster is having a seriously difficult time with conduct, attempt to work in some additional one on one opportunity to interface. This needn't bother with to be a significant length of time, yet it should be regular and centered. Indeed, even 15 minutes per day of committed, telephone free, time with your kid can make your association more grounded than at any other time

3. Be firm, yet all at once adoring

Such a great deal positive nurturing is in the tone. You can be firm and hold your kids to exclusive requirements, while as yet being adoring.

Conclude what rules are critical to you, obviously convey them to your kid, and be steady with implementing those standards. Being a positive parent doesn't mean allowing your kid to mistreat you. It implies attempting to keep a quiet, cherishing tone when your youngster needs updates about the standards.

4. Try not to disgrace

"You're 6 years of age, don't misbehave!"

"Your room is revolting, go tidy it up."

"For what reason might you at any point at any point tune in? It isn't so difficult!"

Have you said those words? These expressions all have a disgracing impact, causing kids to regret themselves. This normally adversely affects a kid's confidence, yet it is likewise not compelling on the grounds that it supports a kid's way of life as somebody who acts a specific way.

In the event that your kid is constantly informed they're misbehaving, they will assimilate this and act that way considerably more. On the off chance that you allude to them as a domineering jerk, they will think about themselves that way and act as needs be. Attempt to remark on your youngster's way of behaving, telling them when it's improper, without prompting sensations of disgrace.

5. Attempt normal outcomes

Rebuffing your kid makes you the foe and can frequently be confounding in the event that the discipline is irrelevant to the offense. Rather than discipline, take a stab at permitting the normal outcomes of their activities to unfurl.

For instance, assuming you request that your baby put on their downpour boots and they deny, the regular outcome is that their feet will get wet outside. They will be undeniably bound to submit next time now is the ideal time to put on boots than if you answer with a break when they say, "no!" to rain boots.

6. Utilize coherent outcome

While normal results are ideal since they don't place you in resistance with your kid, there isn't generally a helpful, transient regular outcome.

For instance, it very well may be essential to you that your kid takes care of each of their Legos consistently so you don't step aerobics them (oof!)

The possible long haul regular outcome would be that a few Legos could move lost on the off chance that they're not taken care of each and every day. This could require weeks or months to happen and your feet probably won't have the option to take that.

In this kind of circumstance, attempt to consider a connected outcome that checks out, and execute it without outrage. The outcome may be that assuming you step on a Lego, you will take care of it in the carport rather than back in your kid's Lego canister.

7. Utilize uplifting feedback

Did your youngster make sure to take care of their shoes without anyone else? Did they help their sister when she was disappointed with her schoolwork? Tell them that you took note!

It's not difficult to remark on awful way of behaving, however grin to yourself when your youngster accomplishes something delightful. Ensure they certainly stand out for good way of behaving than for terrible.

This doesn't mean you want a sumptuous prize framework — simply let them know what you saw. Express something like, "I saw you set your shoes aside without anyone else. That shows genuine obligation!" Or, "I saw you help your sister. You truly care about others."

As well as telling them you saw, this sort of commendation assists your kid with keeping a positive self-character that they will need to satisfy.

8. Model regard

Kids duplicate what we do. In the event that we believe they should be deferential to other people, we must be aware of them.

Assuming you maintain that your kid should say "kindly," say "please" to them.

On the off chance that you believe they should hold on until you're free as opposed to intruding on you, hold on until they get to a place to pause in their play prior to requesting that they follow through with something.

Assuming that you believe they should be thoughtful and delicate with their kin, be caring and delicate with them.

Children absorb everything around them, including how we treat them, even though it can be challenging to put this into practice in our hectic, stressed-out lives.

9. Work to develop empathy

Sometimes it feels like our kids are acting out to inconvenience us. Why don't they simply abide by the park's rules so that you all can have a good time?

However, there is always an explanation for misbehavior, whether it be as straightforward as a child who is hungry or tired, or as complex as issues at school.

Finding empathy for your child and providing a kind response will be much simpler if you can identify the cause of the inappropriate behavior. Just be aware that there is a reason even if you can't identify it. There is a reason why your child is acting out because they want to please you and love you more than anything.

Use time-in instead of time-out.

Building and maintaining a relationship with your child while also bringing up a person who will be kind to others is the aim of positive parenting.

The use of time-outs conveys to our children that we are powerless over their behavior and would prefer to hide their boisterous, irate, and messy side. You are forced apart.

Spending quality time with your child or "time-in" strengthens your relationship. It acknowledges that regardless of how they behave on any given day, all children want to know that their parents love and accept them.

Time spent inside is not always enjoyable. Not everything involves hugs and rainbow-painting.

Because you're maintaining the line on a boundary, it might appear as though your child is sobbing or acting out next to you. It might appear that you are describing the significance of the safety precautions you have taken and the reasons you had to leave the park early.

Time-in doesn't imply that everyone is always happy and smiling, but it does imply that everyone feels loved and that your child knows you will always be there for them and be able to handle whatever they throw at you.

Additional Parenting Skills

1. Your child deserves a lot of tender physical attention

Children enjoy handshakes, hugs, and cuddles despite how simple they may seem. Give them the love they want to receive. It's okay if they don't show excessive affection. Learn your child's preferences for care and consolation.

2. Provide them with a range of activities to engage in

Provide your child with plenty of entertaining indoor and outdoor activities, such as reading, games, puzzles, science projects, nature walks, blanket tents, etc. because bored kids are more likely to misbehave.

3. Set firm guidelines for your child's conduct

Discuss the family rules in your home as a family over dinner. Inform your child of the repercussions for breaking the rules. Few, fair, simple, enforceable, and positively stated rules should be in place (e.g., wash your hands before eating, stay close to dad in the store).

4. Avoid encouraging their emotional outbursts

If your child misbehaves, keep your cool, give them clear instructions to stop, and explain what you want them to do instead. Stop throwing, for example. On the ground, have fun with the truck. If your child stops, give them specific praise. (For instance, "I appreciate you playing with the truck on the ground.

5. Possess reasonable expectations

There will inevitably be some discipline issues because all kids act up occasionally. You might set yourself up for frustration and disappointment by trying to be the ideal parent and expecting your child to behave perfectly.

6. Don't neglect to look after yourself

If you are stressed, anxious, or depressed, it is challenging to be a calm, relaxed parent. Try to carve out some time each day—or at least once per week—to relax or do something you like. Give yourself permission to take time for yourself, even though I understand that it can be challenging as a parent. It affects things.

7. Remember to pay attention to your child when he or she is doing well

Your kids need to be encouraged positively. If they do not get favorable attention from their family, they might decide to seek out negative attention. This is because getting any kind of attention is better than getting none at all. Do not forget to communicate with your child. The most effective healers are love and care.

8. Take into account the flaws and errors of your child

Punishment is less effective for children than praise and rewards. Instead of focusing on your child's shortcomings, figure out how you can best assist them in realizing their full potential. If children are given the opportunity, they will develop their talents to make up for any shortcomings.

9. Don't react emotionally negatively to your child's actions

Negative responses, such as anger, sarcasm, and ridicule, will only make your child feel worse if they struggle with self-control. To help your child concentrate, use short, gentle verbal cues like "L P A" for "let's pay attention.'"

10. Set a good example for your children. (Exemplify what you want)

Consider your children as copycats who will copy everything you do. They will feel free to act badly if they see it from you if you behave badly. Make sure you're okay so you don't explode in front of the kids.

11. Never stop believing in your child

With time, humor, and goodwill, you can solve all of your child's problems. Even the most troublesome teenagers can develop into amazing people with the right parental guidance.

Adopting these suggestions for your family may require some getting used to, but if you persevere, you will be thrilled with the outcomes. We will have much better results and the entire family will be happier and healthier when we incorporate compassion and kindness into parenting practices. When we incorporate compassion and kindness into parenting techniques, we will achieve much better results, and the entire family will be happier and healthier.

How to Handle an Anxious Child (and What Not to Do)

How to respect emotions while not feeding fears

Even the most well-intentioned parents can get stuck in a vicious cycle when their kids have anxiety disorders, and because they don't want them to suffer, they end up making things worse for the kid. It occurs when parents attempt to shield their children from their fears in anticipation of those fears. Here are some suggestions for assisting kids in breaking the cycle of anxiety.

1. Rather than eradicating anxiety, the objective is to assist a child in managing it.

Although no one wants to see a child in pain, attempting to shield children from the stresses that cause anxiety isn't the best course of action. It aims to teach them how to manage their anxiety and carry on as normally as possible even when they're feeling anxious. And as a result, over time, the anxiety will lessen or go away.

2. Don't avoid things just because a child gets anxious about them. In the short run, children will feel better if you help them avoid the things they are afraid of, but in the long run, it will only make their anxiety worse. If a child experiences discomfort and begins to cry—not out of any kind of manipulation, but simply because that's how she feels—and her parents whisk her away or take away the trigger, she has learned that coping mechanisms and the cycle may continue in the future.

3. State optimistic but reasonable expectations. You can't assure a child that his worries are unfounded—that he won't make a mistake on a test, that ice skating will be enjoyable, or that another kid won't tease him during show and tell. You can reassure him, though, that everything will be alright, he can handle it, and that as he faces his anxieties, it will gradually get better. He gains confidence from this that you won't ask him to do something he can't handle and that your expectations are reasonable..

4. Honor her feelings, but don't give them authority.

It's critical to understand that confirmation doesn't always equate to agreement. So, if a child is scared of going to the doctor because she needs a shot, you shouldn't downplay her worries while also being careful not to exaggerate them. Empathize with her, assist her in identifying the cause of her anxiety, and give her the self-assurance she needs to face her fears. You want to convey the idea that, "I understand that you're nervous, and that's okay. I'm here to help you get through this."

5. Refrain from asking for directions.

Encourage your child to express his emotions rather than asking open-ended questions like, "Are you nervous about the big test?" Do you hesitate to enter science fair competitions? To avoid adding to the cycle of anxiety, just ask open-ended questions, like, "How do you feel about the science fair?"

6. Avoid encouraging the child's fears..

The last thing you want to do is convey through your voice or body language that "maybe this is something you should be afraid of." Consider the case where a youngster had a bad encounter with a dog. You might worry about how she will react the next time she is around a dog and unintentionally convey that she should be concerned.

7. Encourage the youngster to put up with her fear.

Let your child know that you appreciate the work it takes to tolerate anxiety in order to do what he wants or needs to do. It's really motivating him to live life and let the anxiety follow its course. The "habituation curve" is what we refer to it as, and as long as he stays in contact with the stressor, it will gradually decline. However, that is how we overcome our fears. It might not drop to zero or drop as quickly as you would like.

8. Make an effort to minimize the waiting time.

The hardest part of facing our fears usually comes right before we act. The anticipatory period should therefore be minimized or eliminated as a general rule for parents. You shouldn't start a conversation about going to the doctor with a nervous child two hours before you go because that will probably only make them more agitated. So simply try to cut that time as much as possible.

9. Talk to the child about the situation.

Sometimes it can be helpful to discuss what would occur if a child's fear came true, as well as how she would handle it. A child who is anxious about dropping her off at school might worry about what would happen if her parents forgot to pick her up. We talk about that here. What would you do if your mother did not show up when soccer practice was over? I'd tell the coach that my mother isn't present, though. And what do you anticipate the coach doing? But he'd call my mom, I guess. He had the option of waiting with me. Young children who are concerned that they might be picked up by a stranger can ask their parents for a code word that everyone they send will understand. Making a plan may help some kids feel less uncertain in a positive, practical way.

10. Try to set an example for effective anxiety management.

By showing children how you manage your own anxiety, you can support them in a variety of ways. If you keep complaining over the phone to a friend that you can't handle the stress or the anxiety, kids are perceptive and they will pick up on it. While I don't advocate hiding your stress or anxiety from children, I do advocate showing them how you can handle it with grace and satisfaction.

Anxiety disorders are a type of mental illness. Anxiety makes getting through the day tough. Symptoms include anxiousness, panic, and terror, as well as perspiration and a racing heart. Medication and cognitive behavioral therapy are two treatment options. Your healthcare provider can create a treatment plan that is tailored to your specific needs.

Are you worried? Perhaps you are concerned about a situation at work with your supervisor. Perhaps you are experiencing butterflies in your stomach while awaiting the results of a medical exam. Perhaps you become frightened while driving home during rush hour, as automobiles zoom by and zigzag between lanes. Everyone encounters anxiety at some point in their lives. Adults and children are also included. Anxiety, for the most part, comes and goes, lasting only a brief time. Some anxiety attacks are more intense than others, lasting anything from a few minutes to a few days. However, for some people, these anxious feelings are more than merely passing thoughts or a tough day at work.

Anxiety disorders are a type of mental illness. You may react to certain things and circumstances with fear and dread if you have an anxiety disorder. You may also notice physical symptoms of anxiety, such as a racing heart and sweating.

It's normal to feel anxious. If you have to deal with a problem at work, go to an interview, take an exam, or make an important decision, you may feel anxious or tense. Anxiety, on the other hand, can be good. Anxiety, for example, helps us recognize harmful circumstances and focus our attention, allowing us to stay safe.

An anxiety disorder, on the other hand, goes beyond the normal nervousness and small worries you may experience. When one of the following occurs:Furthermore, an anxiety disorder transcends the occasional bouts of minor worry and normal trepidation. An anxiety disorder develops when:

When something provokes your emotions, you frequently overreact.

You have little control over how you react to things.

Your response to situations is largely out of your control. Fortunately, there are several effective treatments available for anxiety disorders.

The most prevalent mental health issue in the US is anxiety disorders. 40 million Americans are impacted by them. They affect almost 30% of adults at some point in their lives. Anxiety disorders are most commonly diagnosed in childhood, adolescence, or early adulthood.

When you're anxious or stuck, giving your brain a fast reboot can help clear the backlog of thoughts in your working memory and give you a more organized mental workspace. Consider a desk piled high with snatches of various projects, memos, and crucial papers. When you are looking for a certain piece of information, the clutter might make things tough. Similarly, if you allow superfluous or problematic thoughts to accumulate in your mind, you may find yourself repeating the same unwanted mental material.

When people are stressed, they often discover that their stress is compounded by thoughts about not only the current worry, but also prior occurrences or issues, as well as situations that may occur in the future.

What are the effects of anxiety disorders on children?

It is common for young people to experience anxiety, concern, or dread at times. A youngster, for example, may be terrified of a thunderstorm or a barking dog. A teenager may become concerned about an upcoming test or school dance.

However, youngsters can occasionally approach these moments with overpowering dread or they cannot stop thinking about all the worries associated with one of these. It might seem as though none of your comforts are working. They are filled with overwhelming dread or they can't stop worrying about all the worries connected with one of these occasions. It may appear that none of your comforts are helpful. Daily tasks like going to school, playing, and sleeping are difficult for them. They struggle with daily activities such as going to school, playing, and falling asleep. They are extremely hesitant to explore new things.

"Getting stuck" is important when assessing your child's anxiety levels. It makes a distinction between typical childhood phobias and an anxiety disorder that calls for professional assistance. If fear or worry are interfering with your child's ability to function, it might be time to seek professional help.

Numerous methods exist for diagnosing anxiety disorders.

If you are exhibiting signs of an anxiety disorder, speak with a medical professional. Detailed medical history taking and a physical examination will be the first steps. Lab or scan testing and imaging cannot identify anxiety disorders. To rule out conditions that are the cause of your symptoms, your doctor may nevertheless request some of these tests.

What elements influence anxiety disorders?

Anxiety disorders share characteristics with other mental illnesses. They are not the result of flaws in personality, moral character, or parenting. What causes anxiety disorders, though, is unclear to researchers. According to them, several factors are in play:

Chemical imbalance: Prolonged or severe stress can alter the chemical balance that regulates your mood. An anxiety disorder may be exacerbated by persistently high levels of stress. A lot of stress over a lengthy period of time might contribute to an anxiety condition.

Environmental factors: A traumatic event can trigger the onset of an anxiety disorder, especially in those who are predisposed to it.

The following are the most common causes of anxiety disorders:The following are the main factors that contribute to anxiety disorders:

Anxiety problems are more prevalent in people with a family history of mental health issues. For instance, OCD can be passed down through families. Stressful situations, such as work pressure, the loss of a loved one, or challenging relationships, can cause anxiety symptoms. Medical conditions like thyroid issues, asthma, diabetes, or heart disease can also contribute to anxiety. Anxiety disorder symptoms can appear in depressed individuals. For instance, a person with a long history of depression may start performing below par at work.

What symptoms and signs are associated with anxiety disorders?

Different types of anxiety disorders have different symptoms. Anxiety disorder symptoms in general include:

Physical signs and symptoms:

1. Hands that are cold or sweaty.

2. The mouth is parched.

3. Cardiovascular palpitations

4. Nausea.

5. Feelings of numbness or tingling in the hands or feet.

6. Muscle tension

7. Breathing difficulties

8. Worrying incessantly and excessively for no apparent reason, making day-to-day activities difficult.

9. Fear of any social or performance-related situations in which you may be subjected to scrutiny from others. You are afraid that you will act in a humiliating or unpleasant manner.

10. Irrational fear of an object or location, such as entering an elevator and assuming that there is no way out.

11. Flashbacks, nightmares, and subsequent anxiety as a result of exposure to a very traumatic incident in the past.

12. Cleaning and rearranging things and objects around you in an obsessive and repetitive manner.

13. Rapid heartbeat and laboured breathing

14. Muscle tension has increased.

15. Feeling of tightness in the chest

16. Unsubstantiated and rising concerns, as well as restlessness

17. Obsessing over little matters, which leads to compulsive behaviour

Psychiatric symptoms:

1. I am experiencing panic, fear, and unease.

2. Nightmares.

3. Recurring thoughts or flashbacks to catastrophic events

4. Thoughts that are uncontrollable and obsessive.

Behavioral manifestations

1. Inability to remain quiet and steady.unsteadiness and inability to maintain composure.

2. Performing ritualistic actions, like repeatedly washing one's hands.

3. having trouble falling asleep.

What is the best way for me to deal with an anxiety disorder?

There are numerous methods you can take to deal with the symptoms of an anxiety illness. These strategies can also improve the efficacy of your treatment:

Investigate stress management: Discover methods to control stress, such as meditation.

Participate in support groups: These groups are offered both in-person and online. They urge persons suffering from anxiety disorders to talk about their experiences and coping skills.

Educate yourself: Learn about your individual anxiety disorder so you can feel more in control. Assist friends and loved ones in understanding the disorder so they can support you.

Caffeine should be consumed in moderation or avoided entirely: Caffeine has been shown to aggravate the symptoms of many people suffering from anxiety disorders.

Consult your healthcare provider: Your healthcare professional is a partner in your care. Contact your provider if you believe your treatment isn't working or if you have questions about your medicine. You can figure out how to proceed in the best way possible if you work together.

Eradicate Toxicity

Negative emotional thoughts lead to emotional reasoning which results in bad actions. When you start being overly emotional about something and then you refrain from doing it because your negative thoughts are telling you you are not enough for it.

People are not good with blames because there are two types of people; one who blames others for everything and the second ones who blame themselves for everything. Both kinds of people are negative thinkers because If you are going to blame others for everything then you are not taking responsibility for what you have done while when you are blaming yourself for everything that went wrong then you are harming your mental health and affecting your self-esteem. Fear of failure can hold us back from manifesting our desires into reality. Failure is not something many of us like to confess in a world where meticulously crafted social media feeds show us pictures of perfection and achievement every day. Many of us will go to great lengths to avoid it, focused on the "what ifs" and avoiding any potential disappointments. However, worrying too much about failing can stifle our progress in a variety of ways. We are who we are because of our failures. We often learn far more from our failures than from our accomplishments, and it is this learning that allows us to progress. We genuinely pull back our layers and uncover things about our inner toughness and capacities that we never knew about ourselves in these moments of risk-taking. For some people, the fear of failure stems from a traumatic occurrence in the past. In the past, were you subjected to unfair criticism?

Were you over-expecting, and now the only perfection will suffice?

Have you ever been humiliated in a painful way?

To overcome your fear, you need to ask yourself these questions. It is crucial to be able to distinguish between the present and the past. You can have dual awareness and operate from where you are in your life right now, rather than from the past.

The question is, what is it that is keeping you from taking action?

It is vital to ask questions about this.

Is it a failure to succeed? Or are you being disliked by others?

It is half the battle if you know what is holding you back. Then let them go.

A new experience can have many advantages, so focus on the positives. Our self-esteem and confidence develop when we do new activities, and that we should gently question any inner voices that say otherwise. Our 'edge' is where we challenge ourselves and where we learn the most, so we need to embrace it! This is the stage where things can feel dangerous and unsure and we decide to pull out. The opportunity for progress there, though, if we can start to stay here longer and bear the sense of working at our edge. It's important to have a fear of failure when doing risky things. This does not simply apply to situations where your life is at risk, but also situations where your financial security or mental health may be compromised. Making a move forward should be carefully evaluated in these cases. Consider what might be a real threat. Please remember that we are working at the frontier of our capabilities, not putting ourselves in danger! Think about it, and do not hurry in. As a result, we can select which risks we should avoid and which ones we should take. If you can confidently tell the difference between the two, then you should feel more comfortable taking the risk.

List down your ideal goals and aspirations. Make incremental progress in these directions. As opposed to the end objective, it is the tiny wins, learning and developing along the way that are important to remember. As you begin to encounter varied results, your confidence will grow, as will your flexibility and adaptability. You should ask for criticism and suggestions on how to move forward, and incorporate them as you go.' Being adaptive and overcoming tiny setbacks is much easier than it appears to be.

Reframe your disappointment to help you overcome it. It is a life lesson. Ask yourself what you learned from that perceived failure, and then go forward with your life. Now that you have fallen, focus on getting up. Try to think of ways to approach the challenge with a growth mentality. Depression is a condition in which a person feels sad or hopeless for a long period of time. It's not the same as being sad or depressed. Counseling, medication, or both can be used to treat depression. Sadness, depression, and a loss of interest or pleasure in daily activities are all feelings that we are all familiar with. However, if they continue and have a significant impact on our life, we may be dealing with depression. The following are some of the signs and symptoms of depression: agitation, restlessness, and pacing up and down slowed movement and speech fatigue or loss of energy feelings of worthlessness or guilt recurrent thoughts of deafness.

Social anxiety, melancholy, tension, and low self-esteem can all be exacerbated by negative thinking. To change your negative ideas, you must first understand how you think now (and the problems that result). The secret to altering your negative beliefs is to understand how you think now (as well as the problems that result). You can then use strategies to alter or lessen the effects of your negative thoughts. These actions can be taken as part of a self-help program, but they are typically done in collaboration with a therapist. The tendency to think negatively is fairly typical. You might be thinking negatively because we are more influenced by bad news than by good news, or you might have a bias toward negativity. This could be because it was more conducive to

evolution in terms of survival As a result of cognitive distortions, negative ideas may arise. Certain psychopathologies, such as sadness and anxiety, contain them.

*****

9 789358 053388